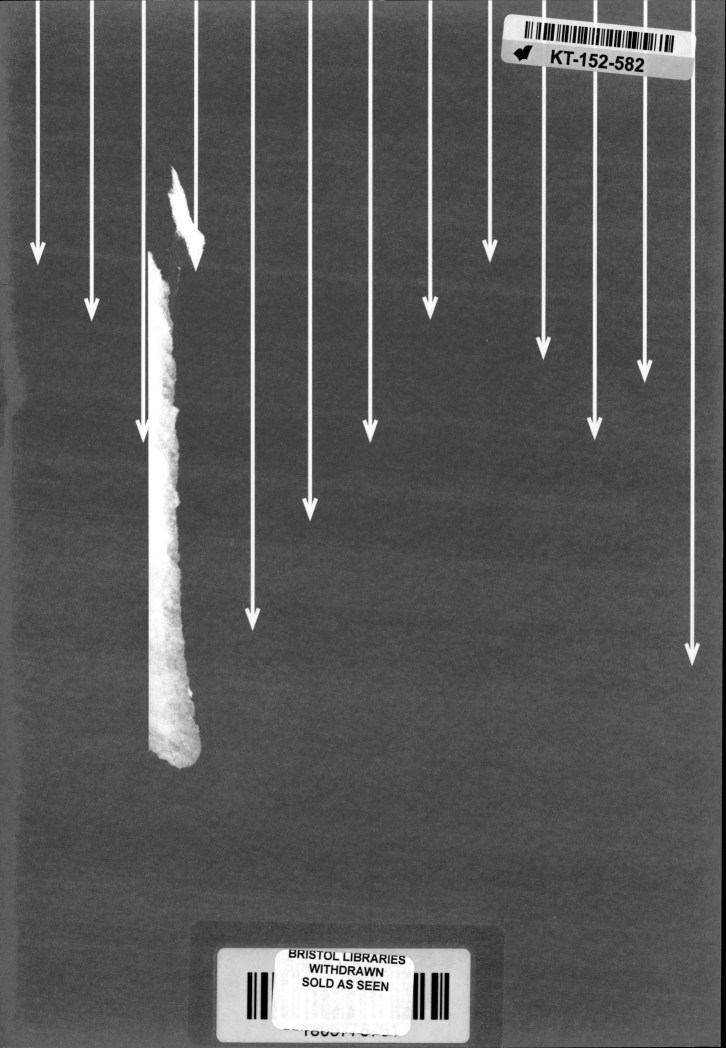

Too good
TO SHARE

Too good TO SHARE

COOKING FOR ONE – 130 CLEVER RECIPE SOLUTIONS

ONE CORE INGREDIENT

TWO DELICIOUS MEALS

SAM STERN

Photography by Lisa Linder

Publishing Director: *Sarah Lavelle*
Creative Director: *Helen Lewis*
Senior Editor: *Céline Hughes*
Designer: *Gemma Hayden*
Photographer: *Lisa Linder*
Food Stylists: *Emily Jonzen and Aya Nishimura*
Prop Stylist: *Polly Webb-Wilson*
Production: *Emily Noto and Vincent Smith*

First published in 2015 by
Quadrille Publishing

Quadrille is an imprint of Hardie Grant
www.hardiegrant.com.au

Quadrille Publishing
Pentagon House
52–54 Southwark Street
London SE1 1UN
www.quadrille.co.uk

Text © 2015 Sam Stern
Photography © 2015 Lisa Linder
Design and layout © 2015 Quadrille
Publishing

Cataloguing in Publication Data: a catalogue record for
this book is available from the British Library.

ISBN: 978 184949 583 7

Printed in China

www.cooked.com

10 9 8 7 6 5 4 3 2 1

A note on the recipes:

Timings are guidelines for conventional ovens.
If you are using a fan-assisted oven, set your
oven temperature approximately 15 °C lower. Use
an oven thermometer to check the temperature.

CONTENTS

6	INTRODUCTION
12	COOK CHICKEN
40	COOK DUCK
54	COOK BEEF
82	COOK PORK
106	COOK LAMB
128	COOK FISH
146	COOK VEGETABLES
172	SWEET TREATS
186	INDEX
192	ACKNOWLEDGEMENTS

SENSATIONAL  SUPPERS

This book is about being creative in the kitchen, cooking what you love and not having to please anyone else! Solo cooks should revel in having the kitchen exclusively to themselves; they shouldn't view it as a solitary experience but a real chance to have fun and experiment. In showing you how to cook for yourself, I hope to be able to inspire you to make the effort – and it's not even a big effort! It's exciting, and much more so than just chucking a couple of boring slices of bread in the toaster. With a bit of guidance, you'll soon get back into the joys of really good food.

The winning idea of this book is that you can make two different dishes from one core ingredient: by cooking the main recipe you are halfway to preparing another, which you can enjoy the next day and even take to work in a lunchbox. This not only saves you loads of time but it also makes financial sense. How often are you left with a lonely chicken breast in the packet and no clue what to do with it the next day? You end up making the same thing again, right? But no one wants to eat the same thing over and over. I want to show you how to solve that problem, and turn it into something different and just as tasty to eat tomorrow.

Sometimes it's also much easier and more economical to buy a whole joint or bird and turn that value-for-money, supermarket offer into a real bargain by creating four separate dishes that will last you over half the week – look out for the Big Cook recipes. This is something I often do myself, and in this book, I'll show you how. There's no magic to it. You can fit it into any routine, whether that means picking bits up from the shop on the way home from work, or booking in a big online delivery and using your fridge/freezer space.

In this book I'll share delicious recipes that are perfect for anyone dining alone, whether that means something quick and easy, or comforting and indulgent. There are some fantastic leftover options, too. Cooking for one shouldn't be apologetic – it's a celebration. For me, whether I've got a house full of people or I'm on my own for the night, I always like to make something delicious to eat. Cooking for yourself gives you more freedom. You are cook and critic. So with only yourself to please, and a stack of great recipes to choose from, you're bound to get rave reviews.

SAM

Kitchen
ESSENTIALS

Of course you can pick up groceries on your way home, or plan ahead on the weekend, but a well stocked storecupboard (and freezer) makes life easy and means a delicious dinner is never too far away. These are my personal recommendations, but you can pick and choose your own favourites.

 ## HERBS & SPICES

Sea salt (I use Maldon)
Fine salt
Black pepper
Vanilla extract
Chinese five-spice
Ground cinnamon
Ground turmeric
Ground cumin
Garam masala
Curry powder
Ground coriander
Nutmeg: whole or ground
Mixed spice
Dried chilli flakes
Chilli powder
Cayenne pepper
Paprika: plain, smoked, sweet
Ground ginger
Dried herbs: oregano, mint, rosemary, thyme

OILS

Olive (for cooking)
Extra virgin olive or rapeseed (for salads)
Groundnut (for stir-fries)
Sunflower (for frying/baking)

MUSTARDS

English
Dijon
Wholegrain

VINEGARS

Chinese rice
Red and/or white
Cider
Balsamic

Chickpeas
Capers
Olives
Chinese rice wine
Coconut milk
Mayo
Tomato ketchup
Brown sauce
Worcestershire sauce
Thai fish sauce
Chilli sauce
Hoisin sauce
Oyster sauce
Soy sauce: light and/or dark
Rose harissa paste
Curry paste (I use Patak's)
Redcurrant jelly
Golden syrup
Runny honey
Maple syrup
Tomatoes: chopped in a can, puréed
Roasted red peppers in a jar
Stock (I use Knorr stock pots)
Couscous (I prefer wholewheat)
Polenta
Lentils
Dried pasta
Noodles
Flour
Baking powder
Bicarbonate of soda
Oats

Beans

Baked
Haricot
Cannellini
Butter
Refried

SUGARS

Granulated
Caster
Soft brown
Icing

Herbs
Chopped spinach
Peas
Berries
Bread: sliced, pitta, wraps
Stock and wine frozen in ice cube trays
Prawns
Squid

Have FUN and EXPERIMENT

Handy tips
FOR BUYING AND STORING CORE INGREDIENTS

 CHICKEN

When buying a whole chicken, look for one that's fat, well-rounded, and neatly shaped. Its skin wants to be creamy and pretty uniformly smooth. Avoid anything with tears, marks, stubble or marks from freezer burn. Check the packaging, too – it should be unscathed. Press before you buy: a properly stored bird should feel cold. Wrap it up in an extra bag when you take it home.

Store raw chicken in the fridge as soon as you get it home – as quickly as possible! Store it in the original packaging or, if opened, on a plate and loosely covered. Keep it away from other foods, especially cooked food. Fresh meat lasts up to 2 days. Top organic meat from the butcher can last 4 days. Follow sell-by dates.

 BEEF

When buying beef, check the colour. You want a deep red with a network or marbling of creamy white fat throughout. It's an indicator of quality, a tender juiciness and flavour to come. If it looks grey, slimy or a uniform bright red colour then avoid it. The fat should be creamy white.

Store raw beef in the fridge: take off any outer wrapping and store it on a plate, loosely covered, in the fridge away from cooked stuff. Meat lasts 3–5 days in the fridge. Cook mince within 24 hours.

 PORK

When buying pork, look for skin that's dry and smooth; meat that's pink and firm without a damp or oily sheen; fat that's white and thick; joints with a good layering of fat (it conducts heat to the skin which helps make great crackling). Avoid meat that looks slippery, and yellow fat.

Store raw pork in the fridge as soon as you get it home: keep it in its original clingfilmed tray. If it's wrapped in butcher's paper, remove it to a plate and cover it with foil or greaseproof paper. When a pack of bacon has been opened, wrap it or store it in a container. Keep raw pork, bacon and sausages away from cooked and fresh foods.

☞ LAMB

When buying lamb, look for good marbling, a firm-textured meat with a pinkish hue, and firm white fat. Avoid it if the meat looks dark and wet, if there's too much fat, or if the fat is yellow and soft.

Store raw lamb in the fridge: keep it in its original sealed container. Transfer open or loosely wrapped lamb to a plate and cover loosely in foil or greaseproof paper. Store away from cooked and raw foods. Refrigerate roasts, steaks and chops for 3–5 days; diced meat for 2 days; mince for 1 day.

☞ FISH

When buying fillets of fresh white fish, the flesh should be white and translucent. Smoked fish should be glossy. Raw prawns should be firm and glistening, with no black age spots. For mussels, try to get ones with cleaner, undamaged shells (not caked in mud or covered in barnacles).

Store fresh fish in the fridge as soon as you get it home – as quickly as possible! Make sure you store it at 0–5°C and eat it within 24 hours of buying. Leave packaged fish in its container, and keep smoked fish well sealed so it doesn't flavour other foods. Allow fish to return to room temperature for 30 minutes before cooking.

 RICE

Make sure leftover cooked rice cools rapidly (don't leave it to sit in a hot pan) and then refrigerate it immediately so it's safe to use. Don't leave it around at room temperature – the longer it stands like this, the more chance of food poisoning from bacteria formed on the cooked rice. Eat cooked rice within 24 hours.

 EXTRA!

Cool hot food down before refrigerating it and make sure it is well wrapped.
Dishes such as curry, stews and casseroles all benefit from chilling for a day or two.

COOK

CHICKEN

BEER AND ORANGE CHICKEN

First off: here's a simple, one-pot, Asian-style dish that I promise you will adore. A light lager works best to create a flavour-packed sauce that absorbs beautifully into the mushrooms and chicken. Second up we have a really light summer salad. Bulk it up with leftovers, like Little Gem lettuce or radishes, tomatoes, etc.

Drizzle of groundnut oil
4 chicken thighs, skin on and bone in
2-cm piece of ginger, peeled and cut
   into thin strips
100ml orange juice
150ml beer (preferably a light lager)
1 tablespoon dark soy sauce
½ star anise
1 pack (250g) shiitake mushrooms
About 60g egg noodles

Put the groundnut oil in a heavy-bottomed saucepan or casserole dish over a medium heat. Add the chicken thighs and brown on both sides.

Pour the excess fat out of the pan, then add the ginger and fry for 30 seconds. Add the orange juice, beer, soy sauce and star anise and bring to the boil. Cover and simmer for 15 minutes.

Meanwhile, prepare the mushrooms by brushing them lightly with kitchen towel to remove any dirt and then slicing them into 1-cm thick pieces. After the 15 minutes, add the mushrooms to the pan and cook for 5 minutes, covered but stirring occasionally. Prepare the egg noodles according to the packet instructions.

For crispy skin, pick the chicken thighs out of the pan and dry the skin with a kitchen towel. Place skin side down in a dry frying pan over a medium heat, or pop under a hot grill until the skin is crisp.

To serve, place your noodles in a bowl or plate, spoon on the mushrooms and cooking liquor and add 2 of the chicken thighs. Allow the remaining chicken thighs to cool, then cover and refrigerate until ready to use in the next recipe.

2 FOR 1

BUY 4 CHICKEN THIGHS, COOK THEM IN THE FIRST RECIPE AND USE THE LEFTOVERS IN THE NEXT RECIPE.

ASIAN CHICKEN SALAD

2 leftover cooked chicken thighs
   from recipe above
10-cm piece of cucumber
2 spring onions
1 tablespoon dark soy sauce
1½ tablespoons sweet chilli
   sauce
1 tablespoon rice wine vinegar
Splash of groundnut oil
Fresh mint and coriander,
   to serve

Remove the bone and any gristle from the cooked chicken thighs. Slice into 1-cm thick pieces. Slice the cucumber into thin batons. Chop the spring onions into ½-cm chunks.

Mix together the soy sauce, chilli sauce, vinegar and groundnut oil to form the dressing. Taste and adjust to your liking by adding more of anything. Plate up the cucumber, then the chicken and spring onions, some mint and coriander leaves, and finally drizzle on the dressing.

CHICKEN TERIYAKI

Chicken thighs are packed with such incredible flavour, and combined with dark, sweet Japanese teriyaki sauce, they are a real winner. The pickles are there to cut through the rich sweetness of the chicken. Surprisingly, this flavouring also works fantastically with nachos, which are perfect for pigging out on while watching TV. (Or you could make your colleagues jealous by including it in a lunchbox.)

4 chicken thighs, skin on (bone in or boneless – see method below)
About 60g white or brown rice
Groundnut or vegetable oil, for frying

Pickles
3 tablespoons rice vinegar
1 tablespoon water
5 teaspoons caster sugar
Pinch of salt
1 carrot
2 pieces of Chinese leaf

Teriyaki marinade
2 tablespoons dark soy sauce
2 tablespoons mirin
1 tablespoon sake or rice wine
1 tablespoon runny honey

For the pickles, put the rice vinegar, water, sugar and salt in a bowl. Stir well to dissolve the sugar and salt. Peel and slice the carrot into thin strips or semi-circles about ¼cm thick. Slice the Chinese leaf to a similar thickness. Place both in the pickle bowl, give them a good mix, cover and marinate for at least 30 minutes.

Now mix the teriyaki marinade ingredients in a bowl.

If your chicken thighs have their bones, remove the bone by cutting through the flesh along both sides of the bone with a sharp knife. Then slice underneath the bone and pull it out. Prick the thighs all over with the knife. Place in the marinade and leave for at least 20 minutes (the longer the better).

Preheat the oven to 200°C/400°F.

Remove the marinated chicken from the bowl and dry the skin thoroughly with kitchen paper. Reserve the marinade.

Heat a dash of groundnut or vegetable oil in an ovenproof frying pan over a medium low heat. Place the chicken in, skin side down, and cook until the skin crisps, taking care not to let it burn. Once crisp, transfer to the oven and cook for 15 minutes, or until cooked through. Meanwhile, prepare the rice according to the packet instructions.

Carefully remove the chicken pan from the oven and place it over a very low heat on the hob. Tip in the marinade and cook for 30 seconds, or until it bubbles away.

Allow the chicken to rest for a few minutes, then slice up 2 of the thighs. Serve on top of the rice in a bowl and spoon over the teriyaki sauce. Add some pickles and get stuck in. Allow the remaining chicken thighs to cool, then cover and refrigerate until ready to use in the next recipe.

2 FOR 1

BUY 4 CHICKEN THIGHS, COOK THEM IN THE FIRST RECIPE AND USE THE LEFTOVERS IN THE NEXT RECIPE.

CHICKEN AND CHEESE NACHOS

2 leftover cooked chicken thighs from recipe left
40g lightly salted nachos
25g Cheddar cheese, grated
2 tomatoes, diced
1 avocado, sliced
Small handful of fresh coriander, torn
Dollop of sour cream (optional)

Preheat the oven to 200°C/400°F.

Slice the chicken into thin strips. Pile the nachos and chicken into an ovenproof dish and top with the grated Cheddar. Bake in the preheated oven for 10 minutes. Pile into a bowl with the tomatoes, avocado, torn coriander and sour cream, if using. Get messy!

CHICKEN SAAG CURRY

This curry is a great takeaway favourite, but even better for being homemade. Using frozen chopped spinach means that you'll only use what you actually need and the rest can go back in the freezer; this a great way of preventing waste. Be aware that the secret of succulent, tasty chicken is marinating – for at least 2 hours, or overnight. The recipe that follows is a healthy kebab – words that don't sit easily together, but it's true!

2 chicken breasts
Glug of groundnut oil
1 medium red onion, thinly sliced
Pinch of salt
2 garlic cloves, crushed
3-cm piece of ginger, peeled and grated
1–2 teaspoons tikka masala paste (I use Patak's)
400-g tin of chopped tomatoes
5 balls of frozen chopped spinach
About 60g white rice
1–2 chapatis
Raita, to serve

Marinade
2 tablespoons tikka masala paste (I use Patak's)
3 garlic cloves, crushed
3-cm piece of ginger, peeled and grated
Juice of ½ lemon
2 tablespoons natural yoghurt

Chop the chicken into bite-sized chunks. Mix together the marinade ingredients in a bowl and add the chicken. Cover and marinate in the fridge for between 2 and 24 hours. The longer you leave it, the better the flavour.

When the chicken has marinated, heat the groundnut oil in a medium frying pan over a low heat. Add the red onion and salt and slowly sweat until the onions start to turn golden brown. Add the garlic and ginger and cook for a further 1–2 minutes, stirring as you go. Then add the tikka masala paste and cook for another minute or so. Add the chopped tomatoes and cook gently for further 2–3 minutes.

Meanwhile, prepare the rice according to the packet instructions.

Put half the marinated chicken plus the marinade in the pan. (Put the remaining marinated chicken back in the fridge, well covered, for the next recipe.) Cook gently for about 3 minutes, then add the frozen spinach. Stir and cook slowly until fully defrosted and well combined, and the chicken is cooked through, about 5 minutes.

Warm up the chapatis in a low oven or in a dry frying pan.

Serve the curry on fluffy white rice with a dollop of raita and the warm chapatis.

2 FOR 1

BUY 2 CHICKEN BREASTS, MARINATE IN THE FIRST RECIPE AND USE THE LEFTOVERS IN THE NEXT RECIPE.

CHICKEN TIKKA KEBABS

Leftover marinated chicken from recipe on page 18
½ red onion, thinly sliced
Handful of cherry tomatoes, halved
1 naan bread or wrap (garlic- and/or herb-flavoured is the best)
1–2 tablespoons natural yoghurt
Sea salt and freshly ground black pepper
1–2 metal skewers

Preheat the grill.

Thread the chicken pieces onto 1–2 metal skewers, shaping the pieces in such a way that they are all roughly the same size on the skewer. Place the skewer under the grill and cook for 10–15 minutes, turning every now and then to get an even cook. Charring is good, so don't worry about that.

Meanwhile, make a quick salad from the red onion and cherry tomatoes and season with salt and pepper. Stick the naan bread or wrap under the hot grill to warm through.

When the chicken is cooked through, remove from the grill (careful – the skewer will be hot!). Slide the chicken from the skewer onto the warmed naan bread or wrap, drizzle over some streaks of yoghurt and eat with the salad.

GRIDDLED CHICKEN BREAST
WITH COUSCOUS AND BLACK OLIVES

Flattened griddled chicken is something I eat all the time, at least once a week – very simple and healthy. You can transform the leftover chicken breast into something spicy, fruity and with crunch – an easy but exceptional lunch. My brother was around when I was testing this recipe and he has since stolen it and takes it into work all the time. Success!

2 chicken breasts, removed from the fridge about 20 minutes before cooking
Squeeze of lemon juice
Olive oil, for frying
100g couscous (I use wholewheat)
150–180ml boiling chicken stock
2 tomatoes
Handful of black olives, pitted
Sea salt and freshly ground black pepper

2 FOR 1

BUY 2 CHICKEN BREASTS, COOK THEM IN THE FIRST RECIPE AND USE THE LEFTOVERS IN THE NEXT RECIPE.

Leaving a good space between them, put the chicken breasts on a piece of clingfilm on a board or work surface. Put a second piece of clingfilm on top and flatten the chicken by bashing and rolling a rolling pin over it. The pieces should end up being about ½cm thick. Place the flattened chicken on a plate and squeeze over a good amount of lemon juice, a grind of black pepper and a drizzle of olive oil over both sides.

Pour the boiling chicken stock over the couscous in a heatproof bowl; the stock should come ¼cm above the couscous. Cover with a clean tea towel and set aside.

Heat a griddle pan over a high heat until it starts to smoke (make sure your extractor fan is on). Season the chicken with salt and griddle for 2–3 minutes each side or until cooked through. Remove and allow to rest.

Meanwhile, once the couscous has absorbed all the stock and is nice and fluffy, add a drizzle of olive oil and some black pepper (the chicken stock will probably be salty enough) and run a fork through it.

Slice the tomatoes. Plate up half the couscous and top with tomatoes and black olives. Add 1 griddled chicken breast and squeeze over a bit more lemon. Allow the remaining chicken breast and couscous to cool, then cover and refrigerate until ready to use in the next recipe.

MOROCCAN CHICKEN SALAD

1 teaspoon rose harissa paste
Leftover cooked couscous from recipe above
Handful of shelled pistachios, chopped
1 leftover cooked chicken breast from recipe above
1 orange, cut into segments

Using a fork, mix the harissa into the couscous. Add the pistachios and mix again. Cut the chicken into strips.

Put the couscous in a bowl and top with the chicken and orange.

CHICKEN LIVER WRAP

I find that liver is sadly underrated. It's cheap, healthy and has a really rich, deep savouriness. You can do both of these dishes at the same time; once the liver is cooked, eat your wrap while warm and then dive straight into the pâté recipe. When I conjured up this pâté in my head, I had no idea if it would work. Turns out it's a delicious alternative to the classic. It makes a lot of pâté, so you should have plenty for the next few days. You can always pot it up into smaller containers and freeze it for another time.

1 pack of chicken livers (400g)
Splash of groundnut oil
2 small red onions, thinly sliced
Pinch of sea salt
2 garlic cloves, crushed
1-cm piece of ginger, peeled and grated
1 tablespoon tikka masala paste (I use Patak's)
50ml water
1 wrap
1–2 tablespoons natural yoghurt
5-cm piece of cucumber, cut into batons
A few lettuce leaves

Prep the chicken livers by slicing them into thirds and removing any white sinew.

Heat the groundnut oil in a large saucepan over a low heat, then add the red onions and salt. Cook until soft and golden brown. Add the garlic and ginger, cook for 1 minute, then add the curry paste and cook, stirring regularly, for a further 2 minutes. Pour in the water and cook until it has almost all evaporated.

Turn up the heat slightly and add the livers. Stir to coat them in the curry mix and cook, turning regularly, until they are cooked through. Take care in making sure that the curry paste does not stick to the pan.

Meanwhile, prepare the wrap by spooning on, in a circular motion, the natural yoghurt. Arrange about one-quarter of the cooked livers in a line on the wrap. Add the cucumber batons and lettuce. Roll it up and it's time to eat. Make the next recipe after if you can – it'll just take a few minutes!

2 FOR 1

BUY 400G CHICKEN LIVERS, COOK THEM IN THE FIRST RECIPE AND USE THE LEFTOVERS IN THE NEXT RECIPE.

CHICKEN LIVER PATE

300g leftover cooked chicken livers from recipe above
About 100g light cream cheese
Squeeze of lemon juice
25–50g butter, melted
Sea salt and freshly ground black pepper

Put the still-warm chicken livers, cream cheese and lemon juice in a food processor and blitz until quite smooth. Season to taste with salt and pepper. For a smoother pâté, add more cream cheese and lemon.

Spoon the pâté into a bowl, allow to cool for 5 minutes, then top with melted butter. Once completely cool, refrigerate and eat within the next few days on crunchy toast.

CHICKEN AND LEEK PASTA

This is slightly healthier than it might sound – but just as delicious! To make it even better for you, choosing light cream cheese cuts down on the fat and the dish works just as well with wholewheat pasta. The second recipe, for frittata, is a wonderful way of using leftover pasta. Serve with a simple rocket and tomato salad and you'll have yourself a hearty, satisfying meal.

2 leeks
2 chicken breasts
Knob of butter
Splash of white wine or Noilly Prat vermouth
100–150g penne
Olive oil, for frying
1 teaspoon chopped fresh tarragon (optional)
2 tablespoons cream cheese
1 teaspoon Dijon mustard
2 tablespoons milk
Lemon juice (optional)
Sea salt and freshly ground black pepper

Put a large saucepan of cold water, with a dash of salt, on to boil for the pasta. Meanwhile, wash and slice the leeks into 1-cm thick rounds. Cut the chicken breasts into bite-sized chunks, about 2cm big.

While the water is heating up for the pasta, put the butter in a heavy-bottomed pan over a low heat. Once the butter begins to foam, add the leeks and wine and cover the pan. Cook, stirring regularly, until the leeks have softened.

Put the pasta in the pan of boiling water at this stage and cook it according to the packet instructions.

Whilst the leeks and pasta cook, heat a little olive oil in a frying pan over a high heat, brown the chicken, seasoning with salt and pepper as you do so. Once it has browned, add it to the leeks and continue to cook until the chicken pieces are cooked through. If you're using tarragon, stir it in now.

Prepare the sauce by mixing the cream cheese, mustard, milk and a grind of pepper. Taste and adjust to your palate.

When everything is cooked, drain the pasta and put it back into the dry saucepan with the chicken and leek mixture and the sauce. Adjust the seasoning, stir and plate up half of it. Allow the rest to cool, cover and refrigerate until ready to use in the next recipe.

Add a little lemon juice, if you wish. The pasta is perfect served with some garlic ciabatta and a glass of white wine.

2 FOR 1

BUY 2 CHICKEN BREASTS, COOK THEM IN THE FIRST RECIPE AND USE THE LEFTOVERS IN THE NEXT RECIPE.

CREAMY PASTA FRITTATA

3 large eggs
Splash of water
300–350g leftover creamy chicken and leek pasta from
*   recipe on page 24*
50g Cheddar cheese, grated
Knob of butter

Preheat the grill.

Beat the eggs and water together. Add the leftover pasta and the cheese and combine.

Melt the butter in an ovenproof frying pan over a low heat, add the egg mixture and cook very slowly. Once it looks cooked about three-quarters of the way through, remove from the heat and stick under the grill. When it has fully cooked and started to turn golden brown, remove it from the grill and slide it onto a warmed plate.

BBQ CHICKEN BURGER
WITH SWEET POTATO WEDGES AND ULTIMATE CHOCOLATE MILKSHAKE

For me, this is just the best. Proper American diner-style food. Nothing to apologise for, just pure indulgence. In the delightful pasta dish that follows, chorizo proves itself once again a staple in the world of leftovers – it packs an extraordinary punch every time and certainly perks up this dish.

1 large or 2 small sweet potatoes
¼ teaspoon hot smoked paprika
½ teaspoon chilli flakes
½ teaspoon dried oregano
Olive oil, for roasting
2 chicken breasts
Squeeze of lemon
1 bread bun
Dollop of mayo
1–2 lettuce leaves
1 tomato, sliced
Sea salt and freshly ground black pepper

BBQ sauce
½ tablespoon brown sauce
1 tablespoon ketchup
¼ teaspoon hot smoked paprika
2 teaspoons honey

Milkshake
300ml milk
4–6 heaped tablespoons chocolate ice cream (Ben and Jerry's Chocolate Fudge Brownie is the best!)

Preheat the oven to 220°C/425°F.

Wash the sweet potato and cut it into wedges. Place the wedges in a freezer bag with the paprika, chilli flakes, oregano, some salt and pepper, and 2 teaspoons olive oil. Seal and give it a good shake to coat the wedges well. Tip onto a baking tray and roast in the preheated oven for 30 minutes.

Leaving a good space between them, put the chicken breasts on a piece of clingfilm on a board or work surface. Put a second piece of clingfilm on top and flatten the chicken by bashing and rolling a rolling pin over it. The pieces should end up being about 1cm thick. Place the flattened chicken on a plate and squeeze over a good amount of lemon juice, a grind of black pepper and a drizzle of olive oil over both sides.

Mix the ingredients for the BBQ sauce. Remove the ice cream from the freezer, ready for the milkshake.

When the potato wedges have about 15 minutes left, heat a griddle pan over a high heat until it starts to smoke (make sure your extractor fan is on). Season the chicken with salt and griddle for 3–4 minutes each side or until cooked through. Remove and allow to rest.

For the milkshake, blitz the milk and most of the softened ice cream with a hand blender in a measuring jug (or use a blender). (If you like your milkshake thicker, add more ice cream and less milk.) Add the last scoop of ice cream but only blitz for a second to keep a few lovely chunks. Serve in a large glass.

Cut the burger bun in half through the middle. Spread the mayo over one side, then add the lettuce, one chicken breast, a smear of BBQ sauce and the tomato. Stack up your potato wedges and enjoy the cooling shake.

2 FOR 1

BUY 2 CHICKEN BREASTS, COOK THEM IN THE FIRST RECIPE AND USE THE LEFTOVERS IN THE NEXT RECIPE.

CHICKEN AND CHORIZO PASTA BOWL

50g penne
100g chorizo
1 leftover cooked chicken breast from recipe
  on page 28
Good drizzle of olive oil
Squeeze of lemon juice
2 tomatoes, quartered
Handful of rocket
Drizzle of balsamic vinegar
Sea salt and freshly ground black pepper
Grated Parmesan, to serve (optional)

Put a large saucepan of cold water, with a dash of salt, on to boil for the penne. Cook the penne according to the packet instructions.

Meanwhile, slice the chorizo and chicken into 1-cm thick strips (or dice the chorizo if you prefer). Heat the olive oil in a frying pan over a medium–low heat, then fry the chorizo until golden brown. Add the chicken, reduce the heat and cook until piping hot.

Drain the pasta and add it to the frying pan. Add the lemon juice, a little more oil, if you feel it needs it, and some salt and pepper to taste. Tip into a large bowl and top with the tomatoes, rocket and balsamic vinegar. Add some grated Parmesan, if you wish.

BAKED LEMON CHICKEN LEGS

Chicken legs done this way make for a harmonious, rounded dish, allowing loads of flavour to be absorbed into the components. It also means less washing up! Watching *The Sopranos* always made me really hungry and this chicken aubergine parmigiana recipe is something Tony would be proud of!

Olive oil, for frying
2 chicken legs
250g new potatoes
1 lemon
6 garlic cloves, peeled
Handful of fresh thyme
150ml chicken stock or white wine
Squeeze of honey
Sea salt and freshly ground black
*   pepper*

Preheat the oven to 180°C/350°F.

Heat a dash of olive oil in a casserole dish over a high heat. Season the chicken legs well with salt and pepper, then brown them all over in the casserole dish. Remove the dish from the heat and put the chicken legs onto a plate.

Slice the new potatoes into quarters, or sixths for larger ones. Cut the lemon into segments, discarding the peel and bitter white pith. Add to the casserole dish with the potatoes, garlic, thyme, stock and honey. Season with salt and pepper and pop the chicken legs back into the dish.

Put the lid on the dish and bake in the preheated oven for 40 minutes. Now remove the lid and cook for a further 10 minutes, or until the chicken and potatoes are cooked through. Allow the chicken to rest for a few minutes. Serve 1 chicken leg in a bowl with the potatoes, garlic and chicken liquor from the dish. Allow the other chicken leg to cool, then cover and refrigerate until ready to use in the next recipe.

2 FOR 1

BUY 2 CHICKEN LEGS, COOK BOTH IN THE FIRST RECIPE AND USE THE LEFTOVERS IN THE NEXT RECIPE.

AUBERGINE CHICKEN PARMIGIANA

Olive oil, for frying
2 garlic cloves, crushed
400-g tin of chopped tomatoes
½ teaspoon sugar
1 medium aubergine
1 leftover cooked chicken leg from recipe left
150g cooking mozzarella
Small handful of fresh basil leaves, torn
Sea salt and freshly ground black pepper

Preheat the oven to 190˚C/375˚F.

Heat a glug of olive oil in a saucepan over a low heat and sweat the garlic for a couple of minutes. Add the chopped tomatoes and season with the sugar and some salt and pepper. Cook over a low heat, stirring regularly, for at least 10 minutes.

Slice the aubergine into 1-cm thick rounds. Season with salt and pepper and brush with a little olive oil. Heat a griddle pan over a high heat and once smoking, griddle the aubergine for 1 minute each side, or until lightly charred.

Tear the chicken off the bone and into bite-sized chunks and thinly slice the mozzarella.

Layer the tomato sauce, aubergine, torn basil, chicken and mozzarella in an ovenproof dish. Bake in the preheated oven for 30 minutes. Serve with crunchy ciabatta, a fresh side salad and a glass of red.

ROAST CHICKEN

A roast is a very personal thing so I'm leaving the accompanying veg up to you... I suggest carrots, parsnips, chicory or some simple steamed broccoli – but you choose! The large quantities of potatoes are needed so that you can use half for the potato cakes in the next few days. Because they've already been roasted, the potatoes and chicken are bursting with flavour, making the cakes super-tasty. Don't skimp on the tarragon, as it takes these potato cakes to a whole new level. You'll also find here two other faves – a selection of incredible sandwiches and a hearty chicken soup which makes enough for a few helpings. I did try to choose just one ultimate sandwich but I couldn't. So I've given you a few of the options I love.

1 large chicken (to serve 3–4, about
   1.2kg)
Olive oil, for frying
Juice of ½ lemon
Fresh herbs, such as rosemary, thyme
   or sage (optional)
4–5 rashers of streaky bacon
   (optional)
450g potatoes, quartered and
   parboiled
Goose or duck fat, for frying
   (optional)
500ml chicken stock
Sea salt and freshly ground black
   pepper

Preheat the oven to 180°C/350°F. Weigh the chicken and work out the cooking time you need – 20 minutes per 450g, plus an extra 20 minutes.

Sit the chicken in a large roasting tray. Drizzle some olive oil and the lemon juice over the bird. Add any herbs you want. Season with salt and pepper. Lay the rashers of bacon over, too, if you wish. Roast the chicken in the preheated oven for the period of time you worked out earlier. With 50 minutes to go, place the parboiled potatoes around the chicken in the tray with a drizzle of olive oil or spoonful of goose or duck fat, and season well with salt and pepper. Baste the chicken every 20 minutes or so and turn the spuds.

To check if the chicken is properly cooked: the leg should be loose, the juices run clear and the meat should be white. Remove the bird and potatoes from the tray and allow to rest in a warm place. Stick the tray on the hob and add the stock. Scrape the bottom of the pan to get all the flavoursome bits involved. Allow to bubble and boil for a few minutes, then decant into a gravy jug. Serve it all up! Allow the leftover chicken (including the carcass) and potatoes to cool, cover and refrigerate until ready to use in the following recipes. Reserve any leftover gravy, too, for the chicken soup later on.

4 FOR 1

BUY A WHOLE CHICKEN, COOK IT IN THE FIRST RECIPE AND USE THE LEFTOVERS IN THE FOLLOWING RECIPES.

CHICKEN SANDWICHES

CLASSIC bread, leftover roast chicken, salt and black pepper, mayo, lettuce, tomato

BBQ bread roll, leftover roast chicken, BBQ sauce, chorizo, cheese

PESTO toasted bread, pesto, mozzarella, cherry tomatoes, leftover roast chicken

TZATZIKI wrap, feta, tomato, tzatziki, leftover roast chicken, radishes, pickled chillies

CORONATION mayo, lemon juice, curry powder, mango chutney, leftover roast chicken

CHICKEN AND TARRAGON POTATO CAKES

100g leftover leg and thigh chicken meat from recipe on page 35
200g leftover roast potatoes from recipe on page 35 (or mashed potato)
Handful of fresh tarragon, finely chopped
A little plain flour
Knob of butter
Sea salt and freshly ground black pepper

Finely dice the chicken meat. Briefly blitz the leftover roast potatoes using a hand blender or food processor until quite smooth. Mix the chicken and potato together with the tarragon and some salt and pepper.

Put some flour on your hands and shape the mixture into 2 patties. Add a dusting of flour on the outside of the patties.

Melt the butter in a frying pan over a low heat. Once it foams, add the patties and cook for a couple of minutes each side or until golden brown. Serve with a salad of tomatoes, rocket and balsamic dressing.

CHICKEN SOUP

1 leftover chicken carcass from
    recipe on page 35
2L water
2 sticks of celery
1 onion, peeled and cut into quarters
Handful of fresh parsley sprigs,
    separated into stalks and chopped
    leaves
400ml leftover gravy from recipe
    on page 35
100g macaroni
Any leftover cooked chicken from
    recipe on page 35, shredded
Veg of your choice, such as frozen
    peas, broad beans, baby carrots
    and/or sliced courgettes

Put the chicken carcass, water, celery, onion and parsley stalks in a large saucepan or stockpot. Cover and bring to the boil. Cook for 50 minutes.

Drain the stock through a colander into separate saucepan. Add the gravy and bring to the boil. Once boiling, add the macaroni and cook until 3 minutes before the macaroni ought to be cooked according to the packet instructions. At that moment, add the leftover chicken and any of your chosen veg.

Ladle into a bowl and sprinkle the chopped parsley leaves over the top. Allow the leftover soup to cool, then cover and refrigerate to enjoy another day.

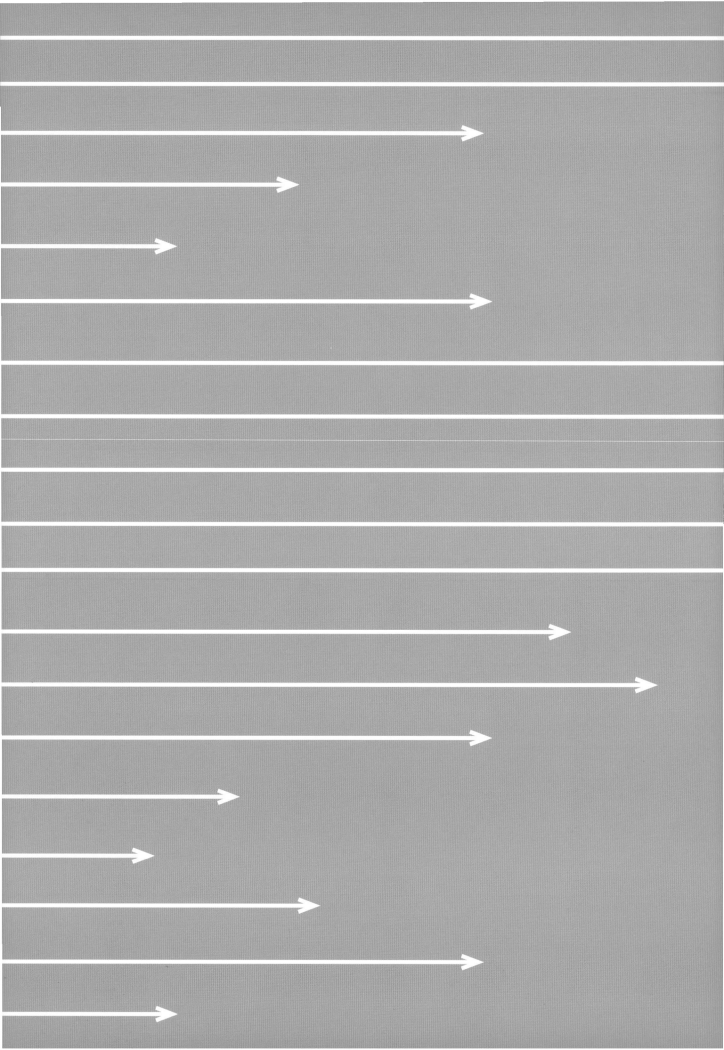

COOK DUCK

FIVE-SPICE DUCK LEGS
WITH CHILLI SWEET POTATO MASH

Duck legs are as cheap as duck gets, but actually they are the most succulent and deeply flavoursome. The sweet potato mash is spiked with chilli and makes a much better accompaniment than the usual old mashed potatoes. The easy soy and honey sauce really hits the spot. For the second recipe, shred the leftover duck and enjoy it in these classic Chinese lettuce wraps.

2 duck legs
1 teaspoon coarse sea salt
1 teaspoon five-spice powder
300g sweet potato
Small splash of toasted sesame oil
3-cm piece of ginger, peeled and
   grated
1–2 pinches chilli flakes or finely
   chopped fresh chilli
2 teaspoons soy sauce
Fresh coriander, torn (optional)

Honey and soy sauce
4 tablespoons rice wine
2 tablespoons water
2 teaspoons dark soy sauce
1 teaspoon runny honey

Preheat the oven to 200°C/400°F.

Place the duck legs in a roasting tray and prick them all over with a fork. Rub the skin with the sea salt and five-spice powder. Cook for 1 hour 20 minutes, draining the fat off as you go (roughly every 20–30 minutes).

Put a saucepan of water on to boil. Peel and slice the sweet potato into 1-cm chunks and boil in the pan of water for 7 minutes, or until cooked. Mash. Meanwhile, heat the sesame oil in a small pan over a low heat, then sweat the ginger and chilli for a few minutes. Add a little water if it sticks. Add to the mashed potato with the soy sauce and beat together with a wooden spoon. Top or mix through with coriander, if you wish.

Prepare the honey and soy sauce by mixing the ingredients together in a saucepan, bringing to the boil and then simmering for 1 minute.

Once the duck has had its time in the oven, remove and allow it to rest for a few minutes. Plate up by creating a pile of the mash, putting one of the duck legs on top and covering with the sauce. Allow the other duck leg to cool, cover and refrigerate it until ready to use in the next recipe.

LETTUCE WRAPS WITH SHREDDED
DUCK AND HOISIN SAUCE

1 leftover cooked duck leg from
   recipe above
¼ cucumber
1 spring onion
3–4 crisp leaves of iceberg
   lettuce
2–3 tablespoons hoisin sauce

Shred the duck leg. Cut the cucumber into matchsticks and finely shred the spring onion. Make up the wraps as you would for crispy duck pancakes: lettuce, a spoon of hoisin, cucumber, spring onion and shredded duck.

2 FOR 1

BUY 2 DUCK LEGS, COOK
THEM IN THE FIRST RECIPE
AND USE THE LEFTOVERS IN
THE NEXT RECIPE.

DUCK LEGS IN PLUM SAUCE
WITH ASIAN GREENS

The duck legs in the first recipe just look after themselves in the oven, so you can focus on getting the tasty Asian greens just right. Remember this way of cooking these greens – they can be teamed up with all sorts of future supper dishes that are crying out for great veg! The leftover duck leg is cleverly reinvented to make a mighty ragu, packed with punch, that can be served with pasta or polenta.

2 duck legs
Good pinch of sea salt
2 tablespoons plum sauce
2 spring onions
3-cm piece of ginger, peeled
2 garlic cloves
1 chilli
1 large pak choi
Toasted sesame oil, for frying
1 tablespoon dark soy sauce
1 tablespoon oyster sauce
Squeeze of lime juice

Preheat the oven to 200°C/400°F.

Place the duck legs in a roasting tray and prick them all over with a fork. Rub the skin with the salt and spoon the plum sauce over them. Cook for 1 hour, draining the fat off occasionally if a lot of it runs off. Then reduce the oven temperature to 180°C/350°F and continue to cook the duck for 10 minutes, basting it well with the plum sauce.

Take the duck out of the oven and allow it to rest for a few minutes. Top with more plum sauce, if desired.

Meanwhile, prep the fresh ingredients. Slice the spring onions into 1cm rounds; cut the ginger into batons; crush the garlic; slice the chilli into thin rings; and chop the pak choi into bite-sized chunks.

Heat a good drizzle of sesame oil in a wok over a low heat and add the spring onions, ginger and garlic. Stir-fry for 2–3 minutes, then add the chilli and continue to cook for a minute. Add the pak choi and soy and oyster sauces. Stir-fry for a couple of minutes until the pak choi begins to wilt.

Plate up one of the duck legs with the Asian greens and serve with noodles, if you wish. Allow the other duck leg to cool, cover and refrigerate it until ready to use in the next recipe.

2 FOR 1

BUY 2 DUCK LEGS, COOK THEM IN THE FIRST RECIPE AND USE THE LEFTOVERS IN THE NEXT RECIPE.

DUCK RAGU

3 garlic cloves
1 carrot, peeled
2 sticks of celery
Olive oil, for frying
150ml red wine
1 leftover cooked duck leg from recipe left
400-g tin of chopped tomatoes
1 teaspoon sugar
2 sprigs of rosemary
About 100g pasta of your choice
Sea salt and freshly ground black pepper
Grated Parmesan, to serve

Crush the garlic, and finely dice the carrot and celery. Heat a good glug of olive oil in a heavy-bottomed saucepan over a low heat and sweat the garlic, carrot and celery for 5 minutes.

Add the red wine and cook until it has reduced down by about half, about 5 minutes.

Meanwhile, take the leftover cooked duck leg and remove the meat from the bone in bite-sized chunks. Keep the bone.

Add the tinned tomatoes, sugar, rosemary and bone to the pan and simmer slowly for 10 minutes, stirring regularly. You will want to put a pan of water on for the pasta at this point; start to cook it at the right moment and cook it according to the packet instructions.

Add the duck to the ragu pan and taste for seasoning. Heat up gently until the duck is piping hot.

Remove the duck bone and sprigs of rosemary. Stir the ragu through the pasta, plate up and serve with a liberal grating of Parmesan.

SMOKEY DUCK BREAST
WITH GRIDDLED ASPARAGUS

Using smoked salt is a great way of imparting a further level of flavour to your duck; it works just as well with steak. Cooking duck this way will render down all of the fat to give you a crisp but fairly lean breast – this then works beautifully in a light and fresh Vietnamese salad that I found on my travels.

2 duck breasts
Smoked sea salt
Small bunch of asparagus
Olive oil, for frying
1 lemon
Sea salt and freshly ground black
  pepper

Preheat the oven to 200°C/400°F.

Heat a dry non-stick frying pan over a medium heat. Score the duck breasts with a sharp knife with a criss-cross pattern and season generously with the smoked sea salt and some pepper. Season the underside of the breast a little, too.

Place the duck breasts, skin side down, into the hot frying pan and cook for about 3 minutes until golden and crisp. Turn them over and sear the other side of the breasts quickly before pouring away the fat. Transfer the duck to an ovenproof dish and roast in the oven for 6–8 minutes depending on the thickness of the duck and how pink you like it. Remove from the oven and allow to rest.

Meanwhile, coat the asparagus in olive oil and a good squeeze of lemon juice, and season with salt and pepper. Heat a griddle pan over a high heat, then add the asparagus and cook for 1–2 minutes per side until charred and cooked. Remove from the pan and squeeze over a little more lemon juice.

Slice one duck breast and plate up the asparagus and your chosen side dish, such as mashed cannellini beans (see page 120) or pan-fried potatoes. Allow the other duck breast to cool, then cover and refrigerate until ready for the next recipe.

2 FOR 1

BUY 2 DUCK BREASTS, COOK THEM IN THE FIRST RECIPE AND USE THE LEFTOVERS IN THE NEXT RECIPE.

VIETNAMESE DUCK SALAD

1 leftover cooked duck breast from recipe left
1 small romaine lettuce
1 small mango
Handful of radishes
Handful of fresh mint, torn
Handful of fresh coriander, torn

Dressing
1 tablespoon sweet chilli sauce
1 tablespoon fish sauce
1 tablespoon rice wine vinegar
½ tablespoon lime juice

Make the dressing by combining all the ingredients in a bowl.

Cut the cooked duck breast into thin slices. Tear the lettuce into bite-sized pieces. Peel and pit the mango and cut the flesh into batons. Thinly slice the radishes. Put the lettuce into a bowl and coat in the dressing. Top with the mango, radishes, duck slices and torn herbs.

ROAST DUCK

Here we have duck three ways, so you can really make the most of a whole duck, which might not be a meat you would normally consider cooking. The whole roast duck in the first instance is a hearty, warming feast; the borek is a tasty Greek temptation made with filo pastry and good for two servings. It can be made as individual parcels, or as one pie. Later on in the week, make the rolls in double-quick time – they are incredibly moreish...

1 large duck
Sea salt
Red Wine Gravy (see page 92)

Preheat the oven to 220°C/425°F.

Stab the duck all over with a fork. Rub some sea salt all over the skin. Put it on a rack in a roasting tray and place in the oven.

After 20 minutes of roasting, reduce the oven temperature to 190°C/ 375°F. Continue to roast until the skin is crispy, the bird is tender and the juices run clear when you pierce the flesh with a sharp knife. This will take about 1 hour 30 minutes to 2 hours.

When the duck is cooked, the fat will have run off into the tray – save it for cooking with another time! It's the best friend a roast potato ever had. Allow the duck to rest for a few minutes.

Carve the duck and set both legs aside for the following recipes. Serve the duck breast meat with the Red Wine Gravy poured over it. Eat with lightly sautéed, buttered cabbage and your choice of potatoes.

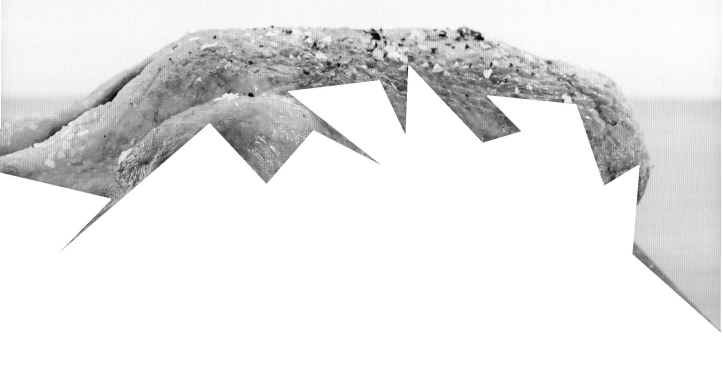

3

BUY A WHOLE DUCK, COOK IT IN THE FIRST RECIPE AND USE THE LEFTOVERS IN THE FOLLOWING RECIPES.

DUCK, FETA AND SPINACH FILO PIE

About 50g butter
125g fresh spinach
1 leftover roasted duck leg from
    recipe on page 49
50g feta
1 teaspoon chopped fresh mint
¼–½ teaspoon grated nutmeg
½ egg, lightly beaten
4 sheets of filo pastry
Freshly ground black pepper

Melt ½ tablespoon butter in a saucepan. Once foaming, add the spinach and cook for a few minutes until wilted. Transfer to a bowl and allow to cool for 5 minutes.

Meanwhile, take the duck leg, discard the skin and shred the meat into small bite-sized pieces. Crumble the feta.

Put the spinach in a clean tea towel and wring out the excess moisture from the spinach. Place it back in the bowl with the feta, duck, mint, nutmeg, egg and a grind of black pepper. Mix and allow to cool further.

Preheat the oven to 190°C/375°F.

Melt the remaining butter.

To make little individual parcels, or borek
Lay the filo pastry sheets out on a board and cut them into quarters. Take one rectangle and keep the others covered with a tea towel to prevent them from drying out. Brush melted butter liberally over the rectangle. Place a second one on top, brush with butter, add a third rectangle, brush with butter and finally top with a fourth rectangle (but do not brush with butter). Spoon the filling diagonally along the middle of the pile of filo sheets. Now brush the edges with butter and fold over the pastry to form a triangle. Place on a greased baking tray. Repeat with the remaining pieces of filo – buttering, stacking, filling and folding. Brush melted butter lightly over the top.

To make one big pie
Grease a small pie dish (about 18cm in diameter and 3cm deep). Lay the filo pastry sheets out on a board and brush melted butter liberally over 3 of them. Stack them up, then lay them inside the pie dish. Let the edges spill over the sides. Spoon the filling in the middle, then fold the filo edges over towards the middle, over the filling. Place the last sheet of filo over the top to cover the pie completely.

Cook the little borek or big pie in the preheated oven for about 15–18 minutes, or until the pastry is well browned.

BBQ DUCK ROLLS
WITH HOT SAUCE

1 leftover roasted duck leg from
   recipe on page 49
BBQ Sauce (see page 28)
1 bread bun
Dollop of mayo
1 tomato, sliced
1–2 salad leaves
Hot sauce (optional)

Pull the duck from the bone and shred it. Mix it with enough BBQ sauce to taste. Layer up your bun with the mayo, salad leaves, duck, tomato and some hot sauce to fire it up.

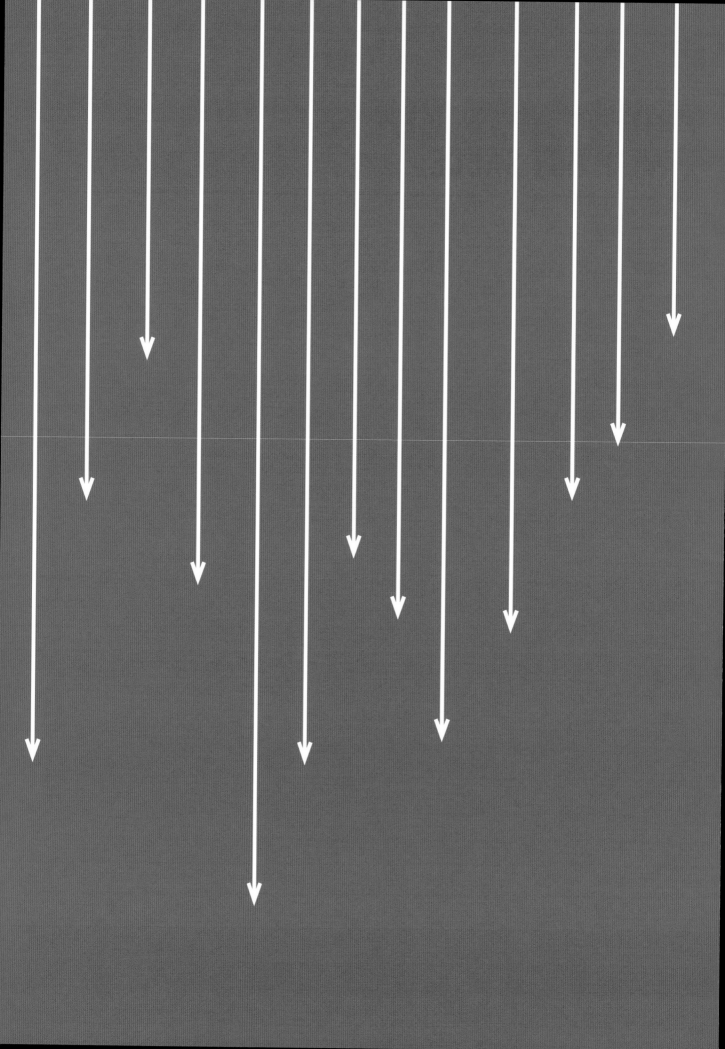

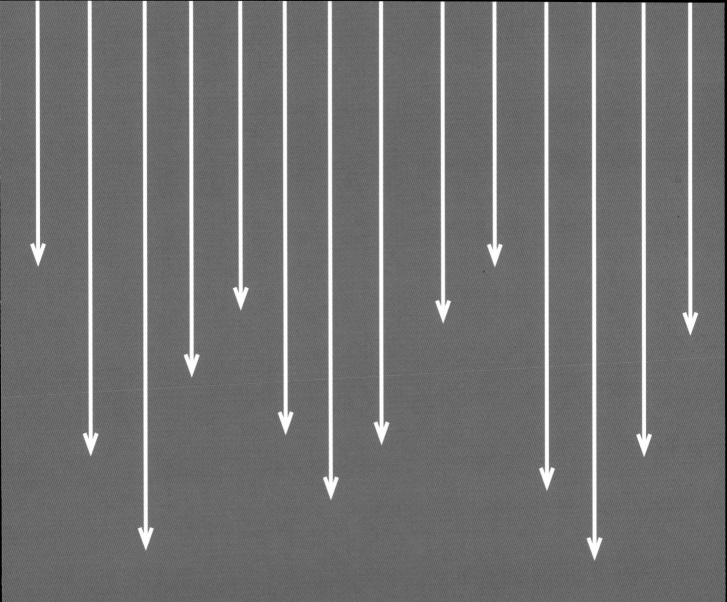

BEEF

PHILLY CHEESESTEAK SANDWICH

This couple starts with a brilliant rump steak. Thinly sliced, it can be as tender as the finest fillet but actually with more flavour. So the Philly sandwich is a real self-indulgent treat – it's the cheese that does it! Its partner recipe, opposite, provides some lighter relief, using easy sweet-roasted peppers from a jar. Together they'll make your steak go further than you could ever think possible. Magic!

1 onion
Butter, for frying
50g cream cheese
50g extra mature Cheddar cheese,
  grated
100g rump steak
Squeeze of lemon juice
Glug of olive oil
1 sandwich-sized ciabatta or sub
Sea salt and freshly ground black
  pepper

Thinly slice the onion. Add a knob of butter to a frying pan over a low heat and once it's foaming, add the onion and a pinch of salt and fry until soft and golden brown, 5–8 minutes.

Meanwhile, combine the cream cheese and Cheddar in a saucepan. Cook over a low heat until it becomes a thick and creamy cheese sauce.

Heat a griddle pan until it is smoking (make sure your extractor fan is on). Trim any fat off the rump steak and slice it across the grain into very thin strips. Put in a bowl with the lemon juice, olive oil and some salt and pepper just before it hits the pan and stir. Cook in the smoking-hot pan for about 10 seconds each side. Remove from the pan and allow to rest.

Cut the ciabatta or sub in half through the middle. Arrange the onion on the bottom, the steak in the middle and the cheese sauce on top. Devour.

STEAK AND ROASTED PEPPER SALAD

100g rump steak
Squeeze of lemon juice
Glug of olive oil
Couple of slices of nice bread (e.g.
  ciabatta)
Handful of mixed salad leaves
2 roasted red peppers from a jar,
  drained
Horseradish sauce
Sea salt and freshly ground black
  pepper

Dressing
1 tablespoon olive oil
1 teaspoon white wine vinegar
¼ teaspoon Dijon mustard
Small pinch of sugar
Pinch of finely chopped fresh
  tarragon

Combine the ingredients for the dressing and give it a good stir.

Heat a griddle pan until it is smoking (make sure your extractor fan is on). Trim any fat off the rump steak and slice it across the grain into very thin strips. Put it in a bowl with the lemon juice, olive oil and some salt and pepper just before it hits the pan and give it a good stir. Cook in the smoking-hot pan for about 20 seconds each side or until it gets a good colour. Remove from the pan and allow to rest. Add the bread to the hot pan and griddle for a minute each side or until it has a good colour.

Toss the salad in the dressing and plate up. Thinly slice the peppers and add to the salad with the steak. Smother the toasts in your preferred amount of horseradish sauce.

BEEF AND ALE PIE

A pair of pub classics. The pie takes under an hour (which is super-speedy for a pie with such depth of flavour) and anything left over, with the addition of cabbage and potato, transforms into gutsy bubble-and-squeak cakes. They're easy to double up if you have enough leftover stew.

300g rump steak
Olive oil, for frying
1 large onion, finely diced
150g chestnut mushrooms,
*   quartered*
Handful of fresh thyme, stalks
*   removed*
About 150ml beef stock, plus extra
*   if required*
150ml ale
½ tablespoon plain flour
Small knob of butter
Sea salt and freshly ground black
*   pepper*
About 100g ready-made puff pastry

Trim any fat off the steak and cut it into 5-cm chunks. Put a heavy-bottomed saucepan or casserole dish over a medium heat. Season the beef all over with salt and pepper and coat it lightly in olive oil. Once the pan has some heat, stick in the beef and quickly seal. Once browned, remove it from the pan and set it aside.

Adjust the heat under the pan to low and add the butter. Once it is foaming, add the onion and a pinch of salt. Fry until soft and golden brown, about 5–8 minutes, stirring regularly. Now add the mushrooms and cook for a further 2 minutes. Then add the stock and the ale and slowly sprinkle in the flour whilst stirring to avoid lumps. Bring to the boil, then add the beef. Simmer, uncovered, for 45 minutes, or until the beef is tender. Add more stock if the sauce becomes a little too thick.

Meanwhile, preheat the oven to 220°C/425°F. Using a rolling pin, roll out the pastry on a floured board to a square 10cm wide and 1cm thick. Place on a greased baking tray and when the beef has just 10 minutes to go, stick the pastry in the preheated oven. Cook for 10 minutes, or until golden brown.

Ladle three-quarters of the beef into a bowl and top with the golden pastry hat. Allow the remaining beef to cool, then cover and refrigerate until ready to use in the next recipe.

2 FOR 1

BUY 300G RUMP STEAK, COOK IN THE FIRST RECIPE AND USE THE LEFTOVERS IN THE NEXT RECIPE.

BUBBLE-AND-SQUEAK CAKES

1 heaped tablespoon leftover beef stew from recipe on page 58
50g cabbage, shredded and cooked
150g mashed potato (use leftovers from another meal, or make it from
   scratch following page 72)
1–2 tablespoons plain flour, seasoned with salt and pepper
Small knob of butter
Drizzle of olive oil
Sea salt and freshly ground black pepper

Chop the bits in the leftover stew into smaller pieces. Combine with the cabbage and mashed potato and season with salt and pepper. Form into a patty and coat them in the seasoned flour.

Heat the butter and olive oil in a saucepan over a medium–low heat. Add the patty and cook for 3 minutes each side or until golden brown and piping hot inside. Serve with a fresh salad.

GINGER BEEF BURGER
WITH ASIAN SLAW

Beef mince is cheap, so go for the best you can find; and 20 per cent fat content will have superior flavour. This burger is inspired by one of my favourite varieties of dim sum – ginger beef balls – and the accompanying slaw adds a real zesty punch. As for the meatballs, their accompanying tomato sauce is a pure Italian beauty that you're sure to fall in love with.

1 tablespoon mayo
Small handful of fresh coriander, finely chopped
Olive oil, for frying
1 burger bun
1–2 leaves of iceberg lettuce
1 wedge of lime (optional)

Slaw
¼ white cabbage, root removed
1 carrot, peeled
¾ tablespoon lime juice
1 teaspoon Chinese rice vinegar
1 tablespoon light soy sauce
2 teaspoons grated fresh ginger
2 teaspoons sugar
2 heaped tablespoons mayo

Burger
200g beef mince
2 teaspoons grated fresh ginger
25g grated apple
25g breadcrumbs, plus more if needed
Small handful of fresh coriander, finely chopped
Grated zest of ½ lemon
Sea salt and freshly ground black pepper

Preheat the oven to 180°C/350°F.

For the slaw, cut the cabbage and carrot into very thin strips using a food processor and shredding attachment, or manually with a knife or grater. Mix together the lime juice, vinegar, soy sauce, ginger and sugar in one bowl. Put the mayo in a separate bowl and stir in the lime mixture gradually to prevent the mayo from separating. Combine at least 2 tablespoons with the shredded cabbage and carrot, but you can add more if you wish.

Combine the ingredients for the burger, season with salt and pepper, and shape into a patty. If it seems a little too wet, add some more breadcrumbs. Refrigerate for 5 minutes. Meanwhile, mix together the mayo and coriander for the filling.

Add a little oil to an ovenproof frying pan on a medium heat. Add the patty and cook for a minute or so on each side until golden brown. Transfer to the oven and cook for a further 5–7 minutes depending on how well done you like it. In the meantime, halve your burger bun and toast it if you like. Spread coriander mayo over one half and add the lettuce. Once the burger has cooked, allow it to rest for a few minutes and then place it on the lettuce. Serve with the slaw and a wedge of lime, if you like.

2 FOR 1

BUY 400G BEEF MINCE AND USE HALF IN EACH RECIPE.

SPAGHETTI AND MEATBALLS

100g spaghetti
Olive oil, for frying
Grated Parmesan, to serve
2–3 tablespoons plain flour, seasoned with salt and pepper
Sea salt and freshly ground black pepper

Meatballs
200g beef mince
25g breadcrumbs
1–2 garlic cloves
2 teaspoons dried oregano
Grated zest of ½ lemon
½–1 egg, lightly beaten

Tomato sauce
2 garlic cloves, crushed
400-g tin of chopped tomatoes
1 teaspoon sugar

Combine the ingredients for the meatballs, adding the whole beaten egg if you feel the mixture is too dry with just half. Season with salt and pepper. Shape into meatballs, roll in the seasoned flour and set aside as you make the tomato sauce. Heat a glug of oil in a saucepan, then add the garlic and sweat it for a bit. Add the tomatoes, sugar, salt and pepper and simmer gently for at least 10 minutes.

Cook your pasta according to the packet instructions. Heat another glug of oil in a frying pan and brown the meatballs on a medium heat until cooked through, or add to the simmering tomato sauce for 3–5 minutes depending on size.

Pile the sauce and meatballs onto the spaghetti and garnish with Parmesan. If you have any leftover tomato sauce, use it another night or freeze it.

MISO STEAK AND CHILLI SWEET POTATO WEDGES

Two more great ways with a rump steak. For the first, the miso adds an exotic sweet saltiness and for the second, the chipotle paste brings a fiery depth that's really exciting and brings the steak to life.

250g rump steak
2 teaspoons brown miso paste
2 teaspoons rice wine
2 teaspoons lemon juice
1 large garlic clove, crushed
Olive oil, for marinating and roasting
1 large sweet potato
1–2 teaspoons chilli flakes
Sea salt and freshly ground black
   pepper

2 FOR 1

BUY 250G RUMP STEAK,
COOK IT IN THE FIRST
RECIPE AND USE THE
LEFTOVERS IN THE
NEXT RECIPE.

Preheat the oven to 180°C/350°F.

Trim any fat off the steak and cut it across the grain into ¼-cm thick slices. Combine the miso paste, rice wine, lemon juice, garlic and a drizzle of olive oil. Add the steak, mix and leave to marinate while you prepare the rest of the ingredients.

Wash the sweet potato and cut it into wedges. Coat in olive oil and season with the chilli flakes and a good amount of salt and pepper. Place on a baking tray and roast in the preheated oven, turning once, for 20–30 minutes or until golden brown.

When the wedges are nearly ready, stick a griddle pan over a high heat (make sure your extractor fan is on). Once smoking, add the steak in batches so as not to overcrowd the pan. Cook for 20 seconds each side, or until it has a good colour. Do not overcook! Remove from the pan and allow to rest in a warm place. Cook the remaining steak in the same way.

To serve, pile about three-fifths of the steak high in the middle on a plate and surround with wonderful wedges. Add a few green leaves, if you wish. Allow the remaining steak to cool, then cover and refrigerate until ready to use in the next recipe.

CHIPOTLE STEAK AND CHEESE QUESADILLAS

100g leftover cooked rump
   steak from recipe above
2–3 teaspoons chipotle paste
2 tortillas (I use seeded
   wholewheat)
3 tablespoons refried beans
50g mature Cheddar cheese,
   grated
Handful of fresh coriander,
   torn
Guacamole, to serve
Sour cream, to serve

Combine the leftover steak in a bowl with the chipotle paste. Allow to sit for a few minutes while you prepare the rest of the ingredients.

Take 1 tortilla and spread over the refried beans. Spread out the steak over the beans and cover in grated Cheddar and torn coriander. Place the other tortilla on top. Heat a dry frying pan over a medium heat. When hot, place the quesadilla in the pan and cook for 1–2 minutes each side until golden and crisp and the filling is piping hot. Remove, place on a board and cut into slices. Serve with dollops of guacamole and sour cream.

BBQ BEEF RIBS

Ribs are a big hunk of meat, deep and rich – and thrifty! This first recipe is for a lazy Sunday when you just want to pig out. It takes minimal effort for such a great result. The second recipe, for the BBQ rib sandwich, is a piece of cake... Ask your butcher to order these ribs in for you. You are looking for 2 ribs, about 18cm long and 7.5cm wide. If you can't get the exact weight or size, don't worry; adjust the cooking time a little to compensate. They are such a good piece of meat...

1.5kg beef ribs
BBQ Sauce (see page 28)

Dry rub
1½ tablespoons hot smoked paprika
¾ tablespoon sea salt
¾ tablespoon freshly ground black
   pepper
¾ tablespoon ground cumin
2 teaspoons chilli powder
¾ tablespoon brown sugar
2 teaspoons cayenne pepper

Preheat the oven to 180 °C/350 °F.

Stick the ribs in a roasting tray. Mix the ingredients for the dry rub and rub generously all over the ribs. If you have any left, store it in a jar for another day.

Roast the ribs in the preheated oven for 3 hours, or until the meat falls off the bone and you can use a fork to pull it apart easily. Slather with BBQ Sauce and serve with a light salad or some buttered corn on the cob. Shred the leftover meat off the rib whilst still warm (it's easier to do this way), then cover and refrigerate until ready to use in the next recipe.

2 FOR 1

BUY 1.5KG BEEF RIBS, COOK THEM IN THE FIRST RECIPE AND USE THE LEFTOVERS IN THE NEXT RECIPE.

BBQ RIB SANDWICH

Shredded leftover beef from
   recipe above
BBQ Sauce (see page 28)
2 lettuce leaves
2 slices of tomato
Bread roll

Stick everything in a bread roll and tuck in.

SPICY STIR-FRIED BEEF

I always seem to make far too much rice, so egg fried rice is a great way of using it up. The secret to storing cooked rice is to chill it as fast possible. As for the first recipe, for spicy stir-fried beef, this is one of my favourites and it never fails to impress and satisfy. Winning combination.

200g rump or sirloin steak

Marinade
2 garlic cloves, crushed
1 teaspoon fresh coriander, finely chopped
1 hot chilli, thinly sliced
2 tablespoons dark soy sauce
1 tablespoon rice wine
2 teaspoons caster sugar
1 tablespoon cornflour

Rice
150g basmati rice
300ml cold water

Sauce
2 tablespoons dark soy sauce
1½ teaspoons sugar
Squeeze of lime juice
Dash of toasted sesame oil

Stir-fry
1 tablespoon groundnut oil
2 teaspoons toasted sesame oil
3 spring onions, cut into 1-cm rounds
Fresh coriander, to serve
Thinly sliced red chilli, to serve (optional)

Trim any fat off the steak and cut it into ½-cm thick slices across the grain. Put it into a bowl with the marinade ingredients and leave it to marinate for at least 30 minutes.

Rinse the rice, then put it in a saucepan with the water. Bring it to the boil, cover and simmer over a low heat for 10 minutes or until the water has been absorbed. Remove from the heat and allow to stand.

Meanwhile, mix the ingredients for the sauce.

Once your rice is under way and your beef has marinated, heat a wok over a very high heat and add the groundnut and sesame oils. When very hot, add half the marinated beef. Do not overcrowd the pan; the steak needs to be brown and cook very quickly to keep it tender. Remove it from the wok and keep it warm while you fry the other batch. Remove that and keep it warm, too.

Lower the heat, add the spring onions and cook for 1–2 minutes. Add all the beef, the sauce and any remaining marinade. Heat for a further minute.

Drain the rice and fluff it with a fork. Spoon half of it into a bowl and top with the stir-fry and a little more coriander and chilli, if you wish.

Allow your leftover rice to cool and refrigerate it for the next recipe.

2 FOR 1

COOK 150G RICE IN THE FIRST RECIPE AND USE THE LEFTOVERS IN THE NEXT RECIPE.

EGG FRIED RICE WITH GARLIC BROCCOLI

½–1 small head of broccoli
200g leftover chilled cooked rice from recipe on page 68
Dash of toasted sesame oil
2 tablespoons groundnut oil
2 garlic cloves, crushed
2 tablespoons hoisin sauce
2 eggs
1 spring onion, thinly sliced
50g frozen peas
1 tablespoon dark soy sauce
Fresh coriander, to serve

Steam the broccoli until almost cooked, 4-5 minutes. Heat the sesame oil and a dash of groundnut oil in a frying pan over a medium heat, then add the garlic and sweat for a few minutes. Once done, add the steamed broccoli and hoisin sauce. Cook for a few minutes until the broccoli is tender. Keep warm while you do the rice.

Beat the eggs in a bowl and add the spring onion. Heat the rest of the groundnut oil in a wok over a medium heat, add the peas and stir-fry for a minute or so until defrosted. Reduce the heat to low and add the eggs and spring onion. Quickly mix with fork or spoon to break it up as it cooks. Before it sets, add the rice and stir well. Add the soy sauce and heat for a minute or two until the rice is piping hot.

Plate up by piling the rice high and topping with the broccoli and a few leaves of coriander.

POSH MINCE AND TATTIES

The trick with this duo is that you can create 2 tempting comfort-food dishes within 2 minutes of each other. Once you've made the posh mince, you put half of it in a dish and top with a mix of mash and cheese. Voilà: cottage pie, ready to be heated up the next day.

4g dried porcini mushrooms
    (about 1 tablespoon)
100ml boiling water
400g beef mince
1 small onion
1 carrot
3 rashers of streaky bacon
1 tablespoon olive oil
Small knob of butter
2 garlic cloves, crushed
75ml red wine
2 tablespoons tomato purée
½ teaspoon Vegemite or Marmite
Small pinch of dried oregano
Small pinch of dried thyme
Sea salt and freshly ground black
    pepper

Mashed potato
800g potatoes
2–4 tablespoons butter
A splash of milk

Put the dried porcini mushrooms and boiling water in a bowl and leave to soak for at least 20 minutes. Take the beef mince out of the fridge to allow it to come to room temperature.

For the mashed potato, peel the potatoes and cut into chunks. Put them in a saucepan of cold salted water. Put this on to boil when you start cooking the mince.

Finely chop the onion, carrot and bacon. Heat the olive oil and butter in a large frying pan over a low heat. Add the onion and garlic and sweat for 5 minutes, stirring frequently. Add the carrot and cook for another 5 minutes, or until it softens a little.

Add the bacon and cook slowly until the fat begins to run. Drain the porcini in a sieve over a bowl, keeping the liquid. Chop up the mushrooms and add to the pan, then increase the heat a little. Break up the mince with your fingers in a bowl. Add it to the pan and allow to brown. Keep the heat low to keep it tender. (Remember to start cooking the potatoes now.)

Add the wine and reserved mushroom soaking water and bring to a low simmer. Add the tomato purée, Vegemite or Marmite and herbs. Stir well. Simmer, uncovered, for about 7 minutes, stirring occasionally.

The potatoes are likely to be done before the meat, so keep them in a warm place or covered with a tea towel. Add the butter and milk, season to taste with salt and pepper and mash well.

To serve, dollop half the mash artfully in a bowl, top with half the mince and add a quick red-wine or redcurrant jelly gravy or a horseradish cream, if you desire.

2 FOR 1

BUY 400G MINCE, COOK IT IN THE FIRST RECIPE AND USE THE LEFTOVERS IN THE NEXT RECIPE.

COTTAGE PIE

Leftover cooked beef mince and mashed potato from recipe left
50g Cheddar cheese, grated

Spoon the cooked mince into a little ceramic dish. Mix the mashed potato with the grated Cheddar and dollop on top of the mince.

Allow to cool, then refrigerate until ready to heat up the next day. Cook in a preheated oven at 200°C/400°F for 30 minutes.

ROAST BEEF

Four beef beauties from one joint. Cook the roast alongside whatever veg you fancy – parboiled potatoes, carrots, parsnips, etc. The other stars here are a classic spaghetti bolognese, a sumptuous gravy-soaked hot beef sandwich, and a refreshing Vietnamese-style beef pho. Remember to keep the gravy from the roast as it is key for the other dishes in place of stock.

1kg beef topside joint
Olive oil, for roasting
500ml water or stock of your
   choice
Sea salt and freshly ground black
   pepper
Horseradish sauce, to serve

Preheat the oven to 230°C/445°F.

Allow the beef to come to room temperature if possible. Rub it all over with olive oil and season well with salt and pepper. Heat a frying pan over a high heat. Once smoking, add the beef and brown the whole joint.

Once browned, remove the joint to a roasting tray. Roast in the preheated oven for 15 minutes, then reduce the oven temperature to 180°C/350°F and cook for a further 30–35 minutes for medium rare, or 45 minutes to 1 hour for medium to well done.

Allow the beef to rest for at least 5 minutes. Meanwhile, add the water or stock to the roasting tray and set over a medium heat on the hob. Scrape any lovely bits off the bottom, bring to the boil and simmer for 5 minutes. Slice the beef and serve with a good dollop of horseradish sauce and glorious gravy.

4 FOR 1

BUY 1KG BEEF TOPSIDE, COOK IT IN THE FIRST RECIPE AND USE THE LEFTOVERS IN THE FOLLOWING RECIPES.

SPAG BOL

150–200g leftover roasted topside
    beef from recipe on page 75
2 rashers of streaky bacon
Olive oil, for frying
1 small onion, finely diced
1 garlic clove, crushed
1 small carrot, grated
1 stick of celery, very thinly sliced
    (optional)
100ml red wine
400-g tin of chopped tomatoes
Pinch of fresh or dried thyme
Pinch of sugar
50–100ml leftover gravy, stock or
    water
About 75g spaghetti
Sea salt and freshly ground black
    pepper
Grated Parmesan, to serve

Chop the beef into very small pieces, roughly ¼–½cm.

Cut the bacon into 1-cm pieces. Heat a little olive oil in a saucepan over a low heat and gently fry the bacon for 2–3 minutes. Add the onion, garlic and carrot and cook for a further 5–6 minutes until softened.

Add the wine and cook gently until it has reduced by half. Now add the tomatoes, thyme, sugar and chopped beef along with the gravy, stock or water if you think the mixture is too dry. Season lightly with salt and pepper and allow to bubble away very gently for 20–30 minutes until the flavours come together.

At this stage, cook the spaghetti according to the packet instructions. Check the bolognese seasoning and serve on the spaghetti. Top with grated Parmesan.

BIG COOK
LEFTOVERS

HOT BEEF SANDWICH

*100ml leftover gravy from recipe on
  page 75, or beef stock*
*100g leftover roasted topside beef
  from recipe on page 75, thinly
  sliced*
Ciabatta bun or equivalent
Horseradish sauce
*Small handful of watercress
  (optional)*

Heat the leftover gravy or stock in a frying pan over a medium heat until just simmering. Add the sliced beef and allow to heat through for about 1 minute.

Meanwhile, cut your ciabatta bun through the middle and spread one side generously with horseradish sauce. Top with the watercress.

Remove the beef from the pan with tongs and place on the horseradish side of the bun. Pour over the desired amount of hot gravy or stock on either just the bottom bun or over the whole thing. This is a knife and fork job.

VIETNAMESE-STYLE PHO

2-cm piece of ginger, peeled
2 garlic cloves, peeled
750ml beef stock
1 star anise
100g leftover roasted topside beef
    from recipe on page 75
About 50g rice noodles
½ red onion
1 red chilli
Squeeze of lime juice
Small handful of fresh coriander,
    torn
Small handful of fresh mint, torn
Fish sauce (optional)

Chop the ginger in half, and bash the garlic with a side of a knife once so it cracks.

Put the stock in a saucepan with the ginger, garlic and star anise. Bring to the boil and simmer, covered, for 20 minutes. Add the noodles to the broth at the appropriate point, according to the cooking time given in the packet instructions.

Meanwhile, slice the beef as thinly as possible, and also thinly slice the red onion and chilli.

Once the broth has had its time, fish out the noodles and put them in a bowl, then cover with the beef. Pour in the hot broth. Top with the onion, lime juice, coriander, mint and chilli. Add a little fish sauce to the broth, if you wish.

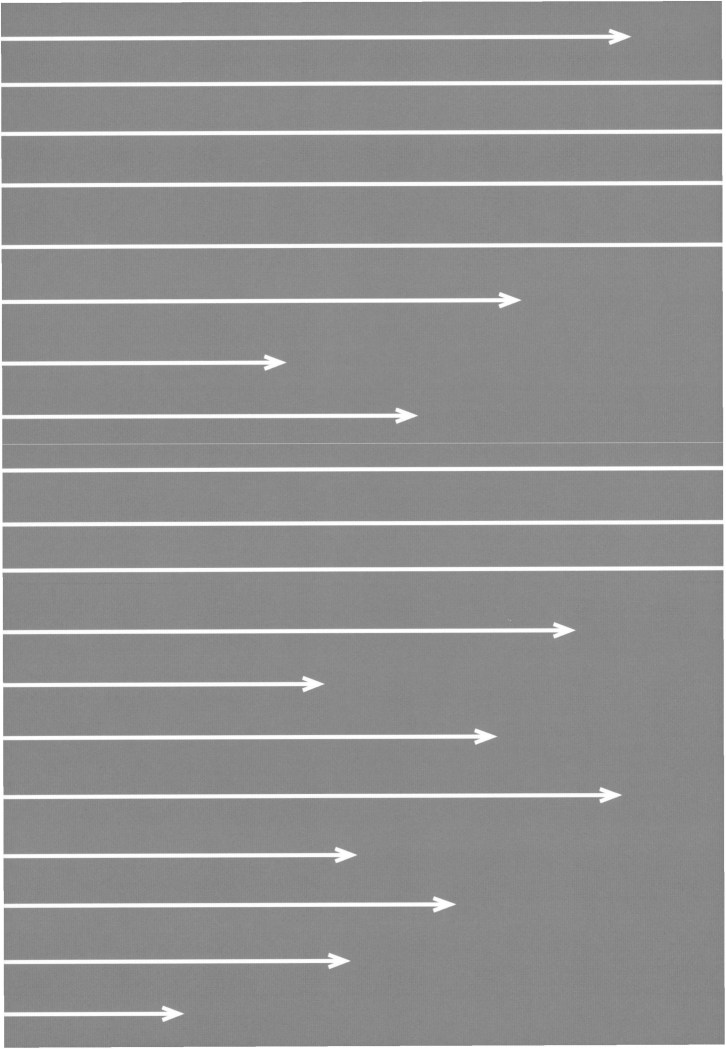

COOK PORK

HARISSA PORK
WITH MANGO AND CORIANDER COUSCOUS

Pork fillet is my Dad's fave because it's a lean hunk of meat, and he's always asking me to cook it, so these pages will have their corners turned down by him for sure! If you have time, marinate the pork for the first recipe for up to 24 hours and it will give it an amazing depth – but it's still fantastic even if you use it straightaway. The key to the leftover stir-fry is the use of dried black fungus, and the chilli and garlic sauce. They will give the dish an authentic taste in under 20 minutes.

2 teaspoons rose harissa paste
Good squeeze of lemon juice
Olive oil, for frying
400g pork tenderloin, at room
    temperature
150ml boiling chicken stock
60g couscous
1 mango, sliced into chunks
Handful of fresh coriander, finely
    chopped
Sea salt and freshly ground black
    pepper

Preheat the oven to 180°C/350°F.

Rub the harissa, lemon juice and olive oil over the pork.

Pour the boiling chicken stock over the couscous in a heatproof bowl; the stock should come ¼cm above the couscous. Cover with a clean tea towel and set aside.

Put a little oil in an ovenproof saucepan on a high heat and add the pork. Brown it off until light golden on each side, then whack the pan in the oven and cook for 8–10 minutes or until cooked through, depending on the size of the tenderloin.

Meanwhile, once the couscous has absorbed all the water and is nice and fluffy, run a fork through it. Add the mango, coriander, a little oil, and season with salt and pepper.

Once the pork is cooked, allow it to rest for 2–3 minutes. Halve it and reserve for the next recipe. Slice the remaining half into rounds and serve beside the couscous.

2 FOR 1

BUY 400G PORK TENDERLOIN, COOK IT IN THE FIRST RECIPE AND USE THE LEFTOVERS IN THE NEXT RECIPE.

SWEET CHILLI PORK STIR-FRY WITH BLACK FUNGUS

5g dried black fungus
200g leftover cooked harissa pork from recipe on page 84
1 teaspoon chilli and garlic sauce (I use Lee Kum Kee)
2 teaspoons water
1 teaspoon oyster sauce
Groundnut oil, for frying

Put the dried black fungus in a heatproof bowl and cover with boiling water. Allow to soak for at least 15 minutes. Meanwhile, slice the pork into ¼-cm wide lengths. Prepare some rice and green vegetables to serve alongside.

Mix the chilli and garlic sauce, water and oyster sauce. Drain the mushrooms and cut off and discard any tough stalks.

In a wok or frying pan on a high heat, add a drizzle of oil. Add the pork and stir for a minute or until hot all the way through. Add the mushrooms and cook for a further 30 seconds. Lower the heat slightly and add the sauce. Stir and cook for 30 seconds. Serve with the rice and vegetables.

CHINESE SLOW-COOKED PORK

This is an easy and authentic Chinese pair. The slow-cooked belly pork is ideal to cook on a Sunday, as it takes little effort but needs a long time in the oven. The salad is a perfect lunchbox bonus for the Monday after.

600–700g belly pork
5 spring onions
5-cm piece of ginger, peeled
4 tablespoons brown sugar
4 tablespoons rice wine
2 tablespoons light soy sauce
2 tablespoons dark soy sauce
150ml water
2 tablespoons groundnut oil

Boil some water in a frying pan that will hold your belly pork and be deep enough to cover three-quarters of it. Add the pork and blanch it in the boiling water for 10 minutes.

Meanwhile, chop the spring onions into 2-cm batons and the ginger into 1-cm matchsticks. Combine with the rest of the ingredients, except the oil, in a casserole dish or heavy-bottomed saucepan.

Remove the blanched pork from the pan and dry it well with kitchen paper. Heat the groundnut oil in a frying pan over a very high heat and brown the pork, skin down, until it is very crisp and deeply golden, about 3–5 minutes. Remove from the pan and set aside.

Bring the ingredients in the casserole dish to the boil, stirring to dissolve the sugar. Add the pork, cover and simmer gently for 1 hour 30 minutes, or until very tender.

Remove the pork from the dish and slice up half of it. Plate it up, pour over the sauce from the dish and serve it with fluffy white rice and simple green vegetables. Allow the remaining pork to cool, then cover and refrigerate until ready to use in the next recipe.

2 FOR 1

BUY A PIECE OF BELLY PORK, COOK IT IN THE FIRST RECIPE AND USE THE LEFTOVERS IN THE NEXT RECIPE.

BELLY PORK SALAD
WITH SPICY SESAME DRESSING

Leftover cooked belly pork from
*   recipe above*
1 garlic clove, finely chopped
1 spring onion, finely chopped
½ teaspoon sugar
2 tablespoons light soy sauce
Drizzle of toasted sesame oil
½–1 teaspoon chilli oil
Handful of lettuce leaves
10-cm piece of cucumber

Slice the belly pork into thin strips, removing the fat if you wish. Mix the garlic, spring onion, sugar, soy sauce, sesame oil and chilli oil together in a small bowl. Shred the lettuce and cut the cucumber into thin batons.

Plate up the lettuce and cucumber, top with the pork and pour over the dressing.

CHOPS, CHORIZO AND CHEESE

Pork and apple are the classic combo here. And then when you smother the chops with cheese and chorizo, it becomes naughty; served with chips, this is proper hangover food! Then the leftover pork is turned into a hog-roast-style sandwich by making the quickest apple sauce ever.

2 pork chops
Olive oil, for frying and dressing
25g chorizo
1 apple, peeled and cored
Handful of raisins
Squeeze of lemon juice
1 slice of Cheddar cheese
Sea salt and freshly ground black
    pepper

Preheat the oven to 200°C/400°F.

Coat the pork chops with olive oil and season well with salt and pepper. Heat an ovenproof frying pan over a medium–high heat, then add the pork chops and brown well, about 1 minute each side. Make sure you sear the fat as well. Stick the pan in the preheated oven for 10–15 minutes, depending on thickness, or until cooked through.

Peel the chorizo and chop it into small dice. Slice the apple into small batons, then mix it with the raisins, lemon juice and a drizzle of olive oil.

One minute before the pork is ready, pile one of the chops high with the chorizo and top with the cheese. Put it back in the oven for the remaining minute, then allow to rest for a couple more.

Pile the apple salad onto a plate with the pork chop on one side. Allow the other pork chop to cool, then cover and refrigerate until ready to use in the next recipe.

2 FOR 1

BUY 2 PORK CHOPS, COOK THEM IN THE FIRST RECIPE AND USE THE LEFTOVERS IN THE NEXT RECIPE.

PORK SANDWICH
WITH QUICK APPLE SAUCE

1 apple, peeled and cored
½–1 teaspoon sugar
1 leftover cooked pork chop from
    recipe above
1 bread bun or 2 slices of bread
Butter, softened

Cut the apple into 1-cm chunks. Place in a microwaveable bowl with the sugar, cover and microwave for 3–4 minutes until soft. (Or, cook it in a pan for 10–20 minutes.) Blitz with a hand blender or food processor, or mash with a fork. Allow to cool, if you wish.

Remove the fat from the pork and thinly slice the meat. Butter the bread, lay the pork on top and smother in apple sauce.

CHORIZO AND SWEET POTATO SOUP

First we have a very simple and inexpensive soup that makes enough for 2 servings – excellent!
Chorizo also plays a starring role in the full-power omelette up next.

400g sweet potato
50g chorizo
Olive oil, for frying
1 small onion, diced
1 garlic clove, crushed
600ml hot chicken stock
Sea salt and freshly ground black
    pepper

Peel the sweet potato and chop it into 2-cm chunks. Peel the chorizo and slice it into 1-cm thick rounds, then slice those in half to make semi-circles.

Heat a little olive oil in a frying pan over a medium heat and fry the chorizo until golden brown. Remove the chorizo from the pan. Throw in the onion and garlic and sweat over a low heat, stirring regularly, for 4–5 minutes. Add the sweet potato, chorizo and stock and simmer gently, covered, for 10–15 minutes until the sweet potato is cooked.

Blend the contents of the pan with a hand blender (or let it cool a bit then process it in a blender or food processor) until smooth. Season to taste with salt and pepper.

2 FOR 1

BUY 75G CHORIZO AND COOK SOME IN THE FIRST RECIPE AND THE REST IN THE NEXT RECIPE.

CHORIZO, FETA AND RED PEPPER OMELETTE

25g chorizo
35g feta
1 roasted red pepper from a jar,
    drained
3 eggs
Splash of water
Freshly ground black pepper
Olive oil, for frying

Peel the chorizo and chop it into small dice. Chop the feta into small dice, too, and slice the pepper into thin strips. Crack the eggs into a bowl, add a splash of water and beat lightly with a fork.

Heat a little olive oil in a frying pan over a medium heat and fry the chorizo until golden brown.

Add the feta and pepper to the eggs. Season with pepper. Tip the egg mixture into the pan over the chorizo and allow to cook, pulling the sides back with a spatula and then tipping runny egg into the space.

When the omelette is cooked through (you can flash it under a hot grill for a minute to brown the top if you like), tip it onto a plate, folding it in half at the same time if you have the knack!

SAUSAGE, MASH AND GRAVY

A firm old friend – absolutely everyone is cheerful about sausage and mash on the menu! The breakfast hash that follows is a hot contender for my favourite-ever breakfast. It is also great for using up any leftovers you have lying around, as it works well with cooked veg, such as broccoli.

6 sausages
550g potatoes, peeled
Olive oil, for frying
Squeeze of lemon juice
1–2 tablespoons butter
Splash of milk
Mustard (optional)
Sea salt and freshly ground black
   pepper

Red wine gravy
1 small onion
50ml red wine
200ml hot chicken stock
1 teaspoon cornflour
1 teaspoon water

2 FOR 1

BUY 6 SAUSAGES AND 550G POTATOES, COOK THEM IN THE FIRST RECIPE AND USE THE LEFTOVERS IN THE NEXT RECIPE.

Preheat the oven to 200°C/400°F.

Cook the sausages on a rack over a roasting tray in the preheated oven for 25 minutes, or until cooked through.

Meanwhile, cut the potatoes into quarters and place in a saucepan of cold water. Bring to the boil and cook for a further 15 minutes, or until they are mashable.

For the red wine gravy, thinly slice the onion. Heat a good drizzle of olive oil in a frying pan over a low heat, then fry the onion, stirring regularly for 10–15 minutes until it turns golden brown. Add the red wine and cook for a minute, then add the stock. Mix the cornflour and water until smooth. Add this to the pan and cook on a gentle simmer for 5–10 minutes or until you're ready to plate up. Season with salt and pepper to taste.

Drain the cooked potatoes and transfer about 150g of them (roughly half a large potato) to a plate with a squeeze of lemon juice. To the remaining potatoes add the butter, milk and some seasoning and mash to your liking. Add a bit of mustard, if you wish.

Plate up 3–4 sausages on top of the mash and cover in gravy. Put the remaining sausages and the reserved potato to one side to cool, then cover and refrigerate until ready to use in the next recipe.

BREAKFAST HASH

2–3 leftover cooked sausages
   from recipe above
3 mushrooms
1 garlic clove, crushed
150g leftover cooked potato
   from recipe above, grated
1 egg
Olive oil, for frying
Butter, for frying
Sea salt and freshly ground
   black pepper

Preheat the grill for the egg if you want it extra fast.

Slice the cooked sausages and the mushrooms into 1-cm thick rounds. Heat a little olive oil and butter in a frying pan over a low heat and sweat the garlic for a minute or so. Add the mushrooms and cook for 2–3 minutes. Add the sausages and warm through for a couple of minutes. Add the potato and cook for 2 minutes until piping hot.

Crack an egg over the top and cook for 5 minutes, or until set. Alternatively, whack it under the grill if you are impatient (and if your frying pan is ovenproof!). Season with salt and pepper and enjoy.

SAUSAGE AND LENTIL STEW

A delightful French winter dish, this stew costs little and is mightily satisfying... And the same can be said for the Italian-inspired sausage pasta. A tasty Mediterranean duo. The best sausages for these, if you can find them, are Toulouse sausages, or those with apple in them.

Olive oil, for frying
3 sausages
1 onion, diced
1 large garlic clove, crushed
100ml red wine
50ml water
400-g tin of cooked green lentils,
  drained and rinsed
Sea salt and freshly ground black
  pepper
Crusty bread, to serve

Heat a little olive oil in a saucepan over a medium heat, then add the sausages and fry until evenly browned. Remove them from the pan.

Add the onion and garlic to the pan and sweat over a very low heat for 4–5 minutes. Add the wine, water, lentils and sausages. Cover and bring to the boil, then simmer gently for about 20 minutes or until the sausages are cooked through. Season to taste.

Spoon into a bowl and serve with crusty bread.

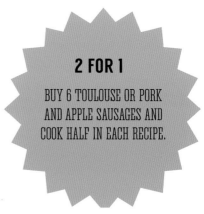

2 FOR 1

BUY 6 TOULOUSE OR PORK
AND APPLE SAUSAGES AND
COOK HALF IN EACH RECIPE.

SAUSAGE AND MUSTARD PASTA

2–3 sausages
1 teaspoon wholegrain
  mustard, heaped
1 tablespoon honey
1 tablespoon orange juice
100g pasta of your choice
1 tablespoon crème fraîche
Squeeze of lemon juice
Sea salt and freshly ground
  black pepper

Preheat the oven to 200°C/400°F and put a large saucepan of cold water, with a dash of salt, on to boil for the pasta.

Place the sausages in a small roasting tray. Mix together the mustard, honey and orange juice, then pour over the sausages. Bake in the preheated oven for 20–25 minutes, turning and coating 3 times until the sausages are cooked.

Put the pasta in the pan of boiling water at this stage and cook it according to the packet instructions to coincide with the sausages being cooked.

Once the sausages are cooked, slice them into 1–2-cm chunks, then return them to the tray and roll to coat them in the honey mixture. Drain the pasta and return to the pan along with the crème fraîche. Stir well to coat, then plate up with the sausages. Add the lemon juice and a grind of pepper.

MAPLE-GLAZED GAMMON STEAK

Gammon steak is thrifty and very tasty. Maple syrup is more than just for pancakes – and here it provides a sweet glaze which beautifully counterbalances the saltiness of the gammon. With the leftovers you can make delicious spaghetti carbonara, which has to be one of the most straightforward yet flavoursome dinners ever.

200g swede, peeled
200g potato, peeled
300g gammon steak
Olive oil, for frying
Knob of butter
Splash of milk
Sea salt and freshly ground black
   pepper

Maple glaze
1 teaspoon cider vinegar
1 teaspoon English mustard
2 teaspoons maple syrup

2 FOR 1

BUY 300G GAMMON STEAK, COOK IT IN THE FIRST RECIPE AND USE THE LEFTOVERS IN THE NEXT RECIPE.

Cut the swede and potato into 1-cm chunks. Put the swede into a saucepan of cold water and bring to the boil. Once boiling, cook for a further 5 minutes, then add the potato. Cook for 15 minutes, or until both the swede and potato are cooked.

Meanwhile, mix the ingredients for the maple glaze.

Lightly coat the gammon steak in olive oil. Heat a frying pan over a medium–high heat and cook the gammon for 1 minutes each side. Lower the heat and baste the steak with a little of the glaze. Cook for 2–3 minutes each side, basting and turning twice. Watch that the glaze doesn't catch, and turn the heat down if it does. Once cooked, baste once more and then allow to rest.

Mash the swede and potato with the butter, milk and some salt and pepper. Cut off about one-quarter of the gammon and set aside to cool before refrigerating until ready to use in the second recipe.

Plate up the remaining gammon and the mash and enjoy!

SPAGHETTI CARBONARA

100g spaghetti
50g leftover cooked gammon
   steak from recipe above
1 large egg yolk
25g Parmesan cheese, grated,
   plus extra to serve
Sea salt and freshly ground
   pepper

Put a large saucepan of salted water on to boil. Once boiling, add the spaghetti and cook according to the packet instructions.

Cut the gammon into small lardons, removing any fat. Once the spaghetti is almost cooked, mix the egg yolk with the Parmesan and a good amount of black pepper. Add a little warm water at the last minute to loosen the mixture.

Drain the cooked spaghetti, reserving the water it was cooked in. Toss the spaghetti with the egg mixture and lardons. Add a spoonful or two of the hot water to create more of a sauce. Serve with a little more grated Parmesan on top.

SAUSAGE MEATBALLS AND PASTA
IN A SPICY TOMATO SAUCE

These two are cheap cheats – they cost next to nothing and are very easy to make. The sausages are transformed into minute meatballs, and the tin of beans takes all the time and effort out of the cassoulet – well, that's just downright cheeky. But it works, so why not!?

Olive oil, for frying
2 garlic cloves, crushed
400-g tin of chopped tomatoes
Pinch of sugar
½–1 teaspoon chilli flakes
½ teaspoon dried oregano
    (optional)
3 sausages
100g pasta of your choice
Sea salt and freshly ground black
    pepper
Grated Parmesan, to serve

Heat a little olive oil in a saucepan over a low heat, then gently sweat the garlic for a couple of minutes. Add the tomatoes, sugar, chilli flakes and oregano and simmer very gently for 10–15 minutes.

Run a small, sharp knife down the length of the sausages and pull off the skin. Divide each sausage into 3 pieces and roll each one into balls. Put a large saucepan of cold water, with a dash of salt, on to boil for the pasta.

Heat a little more oil in a frying pan over a medium heat, brown the meatballs in a little oil. Once the sauce has had its time to simmer, add the meatballs and cook, covered, for 15 minutes or until they are cooked through. Season with salt and pepper. Put the pasta in the pan of boiling water at this stage and cook it according to the packet instructions to coincide with the meatballs being cooked.

Plate up the pasta, spoon over the sauce and meatballs, and be generous with the grated Parmesan.

2 FOR 1

BUY 6 SAUSAGES AND COOK HALF IN EACH RECIPE.

QUICK CASSOULET

Olive oil, for frying
3 sausages (I use Toulouse sausages)
50g chorizo
1 small onion, diced
2 garlic cloves, crushed
100ml cider or apple juice
200g baked beans
¼ teaspoon mustard
50–100ml water
1 slice of white bread
Handful of fresh parsley
Sea salt and freshly ground black pepper

Heat a little olive oil in a heavy-bottomed saucepan or casserole dish over a medium heat, then add the sausages and fry until brown all over. Remove the sausages from the pan.

Peel the chorizo and slice it into 1-cm thick rounds, then slice those in half to make semi-circles. Add the chorizo to the pan and brown, too, then remove.

Add a little more oil to the pan, if needed, and sweat the onion and garlic over a low heat for 4–5 minutes, stirring regularly. Add the cider, beans and mustard and stir. Add the sausages and cook for 20 minutes at a gentle simmer. Stir regularly and add the water if it's looking too dry and sticking. Add the chorizo and cook for a further 5 minutes. Season to taste with salt and pepper.

Meanwhile, blitz up the bread and parsley in a food processor to make breadcrumbs. Preheat the grill.

Once the cassoulet is cooked, transfer it to an ovenproof dish if what it's in is not already ovenproof. Scatter the breadcrumbs over the cassoulet and drizzle with a little olive oil. Grill until golden, then serve.

ROAST BELLY PORK

Here you start off with a delightful piece of belly pork roasted with apples, which become succulent and gorgeous. This is followed by a reunion of the pork and apple in the form of potato cakes – perfect lunchtime snacks. Then for something completely different but just as divine: a satay pork sandwich, the lunchbox king. Finally we've a pork and split pea soup after the Dutch *snert*. My version is a big brassy filler, a winter warmer that's thick and flavoursome from which you'll get several servings.

1kg belly pork
2 apples, cut in half
Sea salt
300–450g potatoes, quartered and parboiled
150ml cider, apple juice or stock of your choice
3–4 fresh sage leaves (optional)

Preheat the oven to 220°C/425°F. Wipe the pork dry with kitchen paper.

Score the pork skin deeply with a small, sharp knife – but not so deeply that you get through to hit flesh – at 1-cm intervals. Place the pork in a roasting tray with room to spare, and rub a generous amount of salt into the skin. Roast in the preheated oven for 30 minutes. Reduce the oven temperature to 180°C/350°F and roast for 40–50 minutes. Now add the parboiled potatoes around the pork and 20 minutes later, add the apples, cut side down. After the time is up, the meat should be very soft and the skin crisp.

Remove the meat from the tray and allow to rest for 10 minutes before carving. Remove the potatoes and apples, too. Pour the cider, apple juice or stock into the tray, set over a medium heat on the hob and bring to the boil, scraping up any lovely bits to incorporate them into the gravy. Boil until reduced by about half and season to taste with salt and pepper. Carve about a quarter of the pork for yourself now, plate up 2 halves of apple, and your roasties. Be liberal with the gravy. Allow the remaining pork and apples to cool, then cover and refrigerate until ready to use in the following recipes.

4 FOR 1

BUY 1KG BELLY PORK, COOK IT IN THE FIRST RECIPE AND USE THE LEFTOVERS IN THE FOLLOWING RECIPES.

PORK, APPLE AND SAGE POTATO CAKES

2 halves of leftover baked apple from recipe on page 100
175–200g mashed potato (use leftovers from another meal, or make it from leftover boiled or roast potatoes following page 72)
50g leftover roasted belly pork from recipe on page 100, shredded
1 teaspoon fresh sage, finely chopped
1 egg, beaten (optional)
1–2 tablespoons plain flour
Olive oil, for frying
Sea salt and freshly ground black pepper

Remove the skin from the baked apple halves and cut into small dice. Combine with the mashed potato, pork and sage, and season with salt and pepper. Form into 2 patties. If the mixture is too dry and won't come together, add some beaten egg.

Put the flour on a plate and dip each side of the potato cake in to coat it lightly with flour. Heat a little olive oil in a frying pan over a medium heat, then fry the potato cakes for 3–4 minutes each side or until piping hot and golden brown.

SATAY PORK SANDWICH

1 bread roll
75g leftover roasted belly pork from
   recipe on page 100, shredded
A few very thin slices of cucumber
Small handful of fresh coriander
A few very thin slices of red onion

Satay sauce
1 tablespoon cider vinegar
1 teaspoon sugar
400-ml tin of coconut milk
2 teaspoons Thai red curry paste
1½ tablespoons smooth peanut
   butter
½ tablespoon dark soy sauce

Mix the ingredients for the satay sauce together in a saucepan over a low heat. Whisk until combined and simmer gently for 4 minutes. Allow to cool if you wish.

Cut the bread roll in half and add the shredded pork, the cucumber, coriander and red onion. Spoon on as much satay sauce as you wish. Eat!

The satay sauce will keep for over a week in the fridge if covered properly; use as a sauce on any meat for a delicious treat.

BIG COOK
LEFTOVERS

PORK AND SPLIT PEA SOUP

1 small carrot
1 small onion
1 stick of celery
Olive oil, for frying
250g split peas, washed
750ml hot chicken stock
75g leftover roasted belly pork from
    recipe on page 100
Frankfurters – 1 per portion
Sea salt and freshly ground black
    pepper

Cut the carrot, onion and celery into small dice. Heat a glug of olive oil in a saucepan over a low heat, then fry the carrot, onion and celery for about 10 minutes or until they start to soften.

Add the split peas to the pan, mix, then add the hot chicken stock. Cover the pan and simmer gently for 1 hour.

Meanwhile, shred the pork. When the soup has been simmering for 1 hour, add the shredded pork and the frankfurter(s) to the pan and allow to cook for 4 minutes.

Ladle into a bowl and serve with a slice of toast spread with mustard. Allow the leftover soup to cool, then cover and refrigerate to enjoy another day.

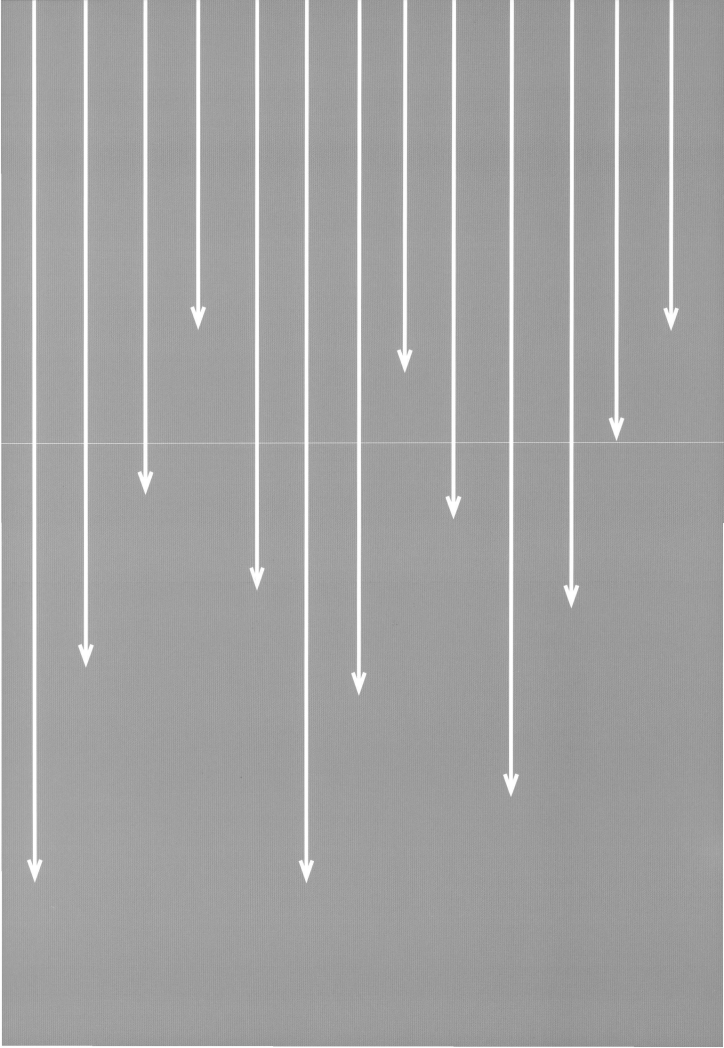

COOK

Lamb

Rack of Lamb
with couscous and griddled aubergine

Rack of lamb is tender, lean and tasty, and cooking it on the bone adds extra flavour. Customise your couscous by improvising with what you have, such as fresh or sun-dried tomatoes, olives, harissa, herbs feta and so much more. In the salad recipe, the Wensleydale gives an appealing flavour counterbalance.

1 small aubergine
Olive oil, for frying
1 lemon
1 extra trimmed rack of lamb, about 300g
150ml boiling water
60g couscous
Sea salt and freshly ground black pepper
Optional fillings (see introduction above)

Preheat the oven to 220°C/425°F.

Cut the aubergine into 1-cm thick slices. Season with salt and pepper and brush both sides lightly with olive oil. Heat a griddle pan until it starts to smoke. Cook the aubergine for 1–2 minutes each side or until golden brown. Remove to a plate and squeeze over some lemon juice.

Pour the boiling water over the couscous in a heatproof bowl; it should come ¼cm above the couscous. Cover with a tea towel and set aside.

Drizzle a little oil and lemon juice over the lamb and season it with salt and pepper. Put an ovenproof frying pan over a high heat, then sear the lamb for 1–2 minutes each side or until golden brown. Transfer the pan to the oven and cook for 9–10 minutes for medium. Remove from the oven and allow to rest for a few minutes. Meanwhile, once the couscous has absorbed all the water and is nice and fluffy, run a fork through it.

Plate up the couscous (adding any optional fillings) and aubergine. Cut half the lamb into slices and add to the plate. Allow the remaining lamb to cool, then refrigerate until ready to use in the second recipe.

Warm Lamb Salad

Big handful of frozen broad beans
Leftover cooked rack of lamb from recipe above, at room temperature
Olive oil, for frying
2 Little Gem lettuces, halved lengthways
25g Wensleydale, crumbled
Sea salt and freshly ground black pepper

Dressing
1 tablespoon natural yoghurt
1 teaspoon white wine vinegar
1 teaspoon olive oil
1 teaspoon finely chopped fresh mint

Boil the broad beans in a saucepan of water for 6 minutes. Drain and run under cold water, then peel each one to remove the pale green skins. Lightly season them with salt and pepper and set them aside.

If you wish, heat the lamb by wrapping it in foil, roasting it at 220°C/425°F for 10–12 minutes, then allowing to rest for a few minutes.

Mix the ingredients for the dressing.

Heat a griddle pan until almost smoking (make sure your extractor fan is on). Rub olive oil over the halved Little Gems and season with salt and pepper. Griddle, cut side down, for 2–3 minutes until golden brown and charred.

Slice the lamb. Scatter the broad beans and Wensleydale over a plate. Top with the griddled Little Gems, lamb and dressing.

2 FOR 1

BUY 300G RACK OF LAMB, COOK IT IN THE FIRST RECIPE AND USE THE LEFTOVERS IN THE NEXT RECIPE.

Shepherd's Pie

This way with shepherd's pie is a completely new invention! Who would have thought a lamb bread-and-butter pudding could taste so good? Magic seems to happen when the lamb juices get soaked up by the bread and the top becomes crisp. Traditionalists can easily top this with mash potato instead. If you had any bits and pieces of veg in the fridge, you could combine them with the onion and carrot and use them up. Turn the rest of the packet of mince into kofta for a touch of the Middle East – especially good for livening up your lunchbox! These recipes are a great lamb mince duo.

Olive oil, for frying
1 small onion, diced
1 small carrot, diced
250g lamb mince
250–300ml beef or chicken stock
1 teaspoon Worcestershire sauce
1 teaspoon tomato purée or ketchup
Butter, for spreading
2 slices of white bread
Sea salt and freshly ground black pepper

Heat a glug of olive oil in a heavy-bottomed saucepan or casserole dish over a low heat, then sweat the onion and carrot for 5–10 minutes until they begin to soften.

Increase the heat and crumble in the lamb mince. Brown for a few minutes. Add 250ml of the stock, the Worcestershire sauce and tomato purée or ketchup. Simmer gently for 20 minutes. Add more stock if it seems dry, and stir regularly.

Meanwhile, preheat the oven to 200°C/400°F. Butter the slices of bread generously on one side, then cut into little triangles.

Once the mince is cooked, season with salt and pepper to taste. Spoon it into a small ovenproof dish and top with overlapping triangles of bread, butter side up. Bake in the preheated oven for 10–15 minutes until the bread is golden.

2 FOR 1

BUY 500G LAMB MINCE AND COOK HALF IN EACH RECIPE.

Kofta Wrap

250g lamb mince
1 teaspoon finely chopped fresh mint
3-cm piece of ginger, peeled and grated
1 garlic clove, crushed
¾ teaspoon ground cumin
¾ teaspoon ground coriander
1 teaspoon mango chutney
1 tablespoon natural yoghurt
1 wrap or pitta bread
1–2 lettuce leaves
1 tomato, sliced
Sea salt and freshly ground black pepper
1–2 metal skewers

Preheat the grill.

Mix together the lamb mince, mint, ginger, cumin and coriander. Mould the mixture into 1 or 2 sausage shapes and thread or shape them around the metal skewers. Grill them for 4 minutes each side or until golden brown and cooked through. Allow to rest.

Combine the mango chutney and yoghurt. Spread on a wrap or inside pitta bread and add the lettuce and tomato. Slice the kofta and add it to the wrap or pitta. Roll or close to serve. This works beautifully with tzatziki.

Lamb and Mint Burger

Cooking lamb burgers this way lets the fat drip away, which is always a bonus. Feel free to experiment with the burger filling by adding cumin, fennel seed or rosemary. With the other half of the mince you can make a brilliant, cheap and authentic curry.

200g lamb mince
1½ teaspoons finely chopped fresh
    mint
50g beetroot, peeled and grated
1 tablespoon natural yoghurt
Squeeze of lemon juice
Rocket, to serve
Tzatziki, to serve
Bread roll
Sea salt and freshly ground black
    pepper

Preheat the grill.

Mix together the lamb and mint and season well with salt and pepper. Shape into a patty. Place on a rack over a roasting tray and grill for 5–7 minutes each side until golden brown and cooked through. Allow to rest.

Combine the beetroot, yoghurt and lemon and season to taste with salt and pepper.

Construct your burger: rocket, lamb burger and tzatziki piled into the bread roll.

2 FOR 1

BUY 500G LAMB MINCE
AND COOK HALF IN EACH
RECIPE.

Lamb Keema Curry

Groundnut oil, for frying
1 red onion, thinly sliced
2 garlic cloves, crushed
3-cm piece of ginger, peeled and
    grated
1½–2 tablespoons balti paste
300g lamb mince
150ml water
Handful of frozen peas
1 tablespoon Greek yoghurt
Squeeze of lemon juice
Sea salt and freshly ground black
    pepper
Fresh coriander, to serve

Heat a little groundnut oil in a saucepan over a low heat, then gently fry the red onion for 10–15 minutes. Add the garlic, ginger and balti paste and cook for another 2 minutes. Add 50ml of the water and cook until it has evaporated.

Increase the heat and crumble in the lamb mince. Brown for a few minutes. Add the remaining 100ml water, cover and simmer gently for 20 minutes.

Add the peas to the pan and cook for 2 minutes. Remove the pan from the heat and stir in the yoghurt and lemon juice. Season to taste with salt and pepper. Serve topped with fresh coriander and accompanied by rice or naan bread.

Garlic and Lemon Chops

First up here is a summery fresh-flavoured treat from the Med. Cooking the chops under the grill gives a hint of BBQ without the fuss. For the other dish, you've pretty much got an instant Chinese delight; super quick and really tasty.

4 lamb chops
2 garlic cloves, crushed
Juice of ½ lemon
Olive oil, for marinating and dressing
60g couscous
80–120ml hot chicken stock
2 teaspoons chopped fresh basil
1 tablespoon black olives, pitted and chopped
Sea salt and freshly ground black pepper

Preheat the grill to its highest setting if you are not marinating the lamb overnight.

Put the lamb chops in a shallow bowl with the garlic, lemon juice and a drizzle of olive oil. Make sure the chops are well coated in the ingredients, then prepare to cook them straightaway, or cover and leave to marinate for up to 24 hours in the fridge. Season the chops with salt and pepper just before cooking.

Put the couscous in a heatproof bowl and pour the hot chicken stock over making sure that it's just a few millimetres above the level of the couscous. Cover with a clean tea towel and set to one side.

Grill the lamb chops for 4–5 minutes each side until golden brown and cooked to your liking. Allow to rest.

Once the couscous has been steaming for at least 6 minutes, run a fork through it until it's nice and fluffy. Add a drizzle of oil, the basil and black olives and season to taste with salt and pepper.

Pile your couscous high and position 2 of the chops on top. Squeeze over a little more lemon, if you wish. Serve with tomatoes, salad or a mix of roasted veg. Allow the remaining 2 chops to cook, then cover and refrigerate until ready to use in the next recipe.

2 FOR 1

BUY 4 LAMB CHOPS, COOK THEM IN THE FIRST RECIPE AND USE THE LEFTOVERS IN THE NEXT RECIPE.

Lamb Stir-Fry

2 leftover cooked lamb chops from recipe above
4 spring onions
2-cm piece of ginger
Groundnut oil, for frying
2 garlic cloves, crushed
2 tablespoons hoisin sauce

Remove the meat from the leftover lamb chops and cut into thin slices. Cut the spring onions into 2-cm batons. Peel and slice the ginger into thin batons, too.

Add a good glug of groundnut oil to a wok or large frying pan. Once hot, stir-fry the ginger for a couple of minutes. Then add the spring onions and garlic and continue to cook for another 2 minutes. Add the lamb, fry for a minute, then add the hoisin sauce and cook for a further 30 seconds. Serve on rice.

One-Pot Lamb Stew

Neck fillet needs some clever slow-cooking, but it's dirt cheap and the results are worth it. The spring broth you make with the leftovers, on the other hand, is very quick – a sheer delight ready in just 5 minutes...

500g neck fillet
2 tablespoons plain flour, seasoned
    with salt and pepper
Olive oil, for frying
1 small onion, diced
1 garlic clove, crushed
1 small carrot, diced
100ml white wine
200g new potatoes, scrubbed and
    halved
3–4 sprigs of fresh rosemary
250ml chicken stock
Lemon juice (optional)
Sea salt and freshly ground black
    pepper

Preheat the oven to 170˚C/325˚F.

Chop the lamb into 2.5-cm chunks and dust them in the seasoned flour. Heat a glug of olive oil in a casserole dish over a medium–high heat and add the chunks of lamb in batches (so as not to overcrowd the dish). Brown them well all over, then remove those chunks, add a little more oil if necessary and sear the remaining batches in the same way. Set all the lamb aside.

In the same dish, heat a glug more oil, then sweat the onion, garlic and carrot for 5 minutes. Add the wine and deglaze the pan for 2 minutes – i.e. scrape any bits off the bottom with a wooden spoon to release all those flavourful little morsels of meat and veg.

Add the potatoes, rosemary, stock and seared chunks of lamb. Bring to the boil then cook at a gentle simmer, covered, for 1 hour 30 minutes, or until the lamb is incredibly soft. Season with salt and pepper to taste and add a squeeze of lemon juice, if you desire. Plate up, setting aside 5–6 chunks of lamb (and a few bits of the veg if you fancy). Allow to cool, then cover and refrigerate until ready to use in the next recipe.

Spring Broth with Lamb

500ml chicken stock
2 handfuls of chopped kale
100g leftover cooked lamb from recipe
  left
Leftover cooked carrots from recipe
  left (optional)
Leftover cooked potatoes from recipe
  left (optional)
Handful of frozen peas

Put the chicken stock in a saucepan and bring to a simmer. Add the kale and cook for about 5 minutes, or until tender.

Meanwhile cut the lamb into smaller chunks and add it to the pan along with any leftover cooked veg. Simmer for another minute. Finally, add the frozen peas and cook for 30 seconds. Ladle into a bowl and serve.

2 FOR 1

BUY 500G NECK FILLET, COOK IT IN THE FIRST RECIPE AND USE THE LEFTOVERS IN THE NEXT RECIPE.

Tikka Lamb Chops

Because the lamb and potato are cooked together in this first recipe, the delicious marinated lamb juices are soaked up by the potato and give them a real intensity of flavour. The spiced shallots in the partner recipe are a pickle-tray classic and have a lovely sharp sweetness.

1 tablespoon natural yoghurt
3 teaspoons tikka masala paste
Good squeeze of lemon juice
4 lamb chops
200g potato, peeled
Groundnut oil, for frying
Pinch of mustard seeds
¼ teaspoon ground turmeric
¼ teaspoon chilli powder
50ml water
Sea salt and freshly ground black
    pepper

Combine the yoghurt, tikka masala paste and lemon juice in a shallow bowl. Add the lamb chops and make sure they're well coated in the ingredients. Cover and leave to marinate for at least 30 minutes, or for up to 24 hours in the fridge.

Preheat the oven to 180°C/350°F. Chop the potato into 1-cm dice.

Heat a good glug of groundnut oil in an ovenproof frying pan over a high heat. Add the lamb chops and fry for a couple of minutes each side until golden brown. Remove and set aside. Wipe any charred bits from the pan.

Heat 2 tablespoons of the oil in the same pan. Add the mustard seeds, turmeric and chilli when it's hot enough (you can tell if it is by adding one seed; if it pops it's ready). Fry for a minute, stirring as you do. Add the potatoes, stir to coat them in the spices and season with salt and pepper. Fry them for 5–10 minutes until crisp and brown on all sides.

Add the water to the pan and turn off the heat. Place the chops on top and put the pan into the preheated oven. Roast for 14–18 minutes, or until the potatoes and lamb are cooked. Finish with a squeeze more lemon juice, to taste. Serve up 2 of the chops on the potatoes. Allow the remaining lamb chops to cool, then cover and refrigerate until ready to use in the next recipe.

Lamb Potato Cakes

2 leftover cooked lamb chops
Groundnut oil, for frying
1 teaspoon tikka masala paste
1 teaspoon garam masala
Large handful of frozen peas
300g mashed potato (use
    leftovers from another meal,
    or make it from scratch
    following page 72)
Beaten egg, to bind (optional)
2 tablespoons plain flour,
    seasoned with salt and
    pepper
Sea salt and freshly ground
    black pepper

Spiced shallots
1 shallot, diced
3 tablespoons tomato ketchup
2 teaspoons mint sauce
1 tablespoon mango chutney
Pinch of salt

Combine the ingredients for the spiced shallots and set aside.

Remove the meat from the leftover lamb chops and chop finely.

Heat a little groundnut oil in a saucepan over a medium heat and add the tikka masala paste and garam masala. Stir-fry for a minute or so, then add the peas and cook for another minute.

Now add the mashed potato to the pan, remove from the heat and stir to ensure everything is evenly incorporated. Add the chopped lamb and season with salt and pepper. Form the mixture into 2–3 patties, adding the beaten egg if the mixture is too dry to bind.

Coat the patties all over in the seasoned flour. Heat a splash of groundnut oil in a frying pan over a medium heat, then fry the patties for 4–5 minutes each side or until golden brown. Serve alongside the spiced shallots and a salad, if you like.

2 FOR 1

BUY 4 LAMB CHOPS, COOK THEM IN THE FIRST RECIPE AND USE THE LEFTOVERS IN THE NEXT RECIPE.

Lamb Steaks
with rosemary cannellini beans

Lamb steaks are relatively cheap, but they can be just as tasty as prime beef steaks if treated with respect. In the first recipe, the beans take on the rosemary extremely well, and they can be mashed if you like, for a nice alternative to mashed potato. Since you've already done the hard work cooking the lamb, the salad in the second recipe is super speedy, needing only that you add feta, rocket and peppers

2 x 225g lamb steaks
Olive oil, for frying and drizzling
1 small onion, diced
2 garlic cloves, crushed
1 teaspoon dried rosemary
400-g tin of cannellini beans, rinsed
   and drained
200–250ml water
Sea salt and freshly ground black
   pepper

Rub the steaks with olive oil and season with a generous amount of salt and pepper. Heat a frying pan over a high heat and, when hot, add the steaks and sear for 2 minutes each side, or until well coloured. Remove and set aside.

Pour away any excess oil from the pan, then add the onion, garlic and rosemary and sweat over a low heat until the onion is soft, about 5 minutes. Add the beans and 150ml water. Simmer gently for 4 minutes. If the pan looks a bit dry, then add a little more water.

Add both lamb steaks to the pan along with any juices that have run off. Cover and cook for 4–6 minutes depending on the thickness of the meat and adding a little more water if the pan looks like it is boiling dry.

Remove the steaks to a plate and allow them to rest for a few minutes. Plate up half the beans and reserve the rest for the next recipe. Slice one of the steaks and rest on top of the plate of beans. Reserve the second steak for the next recipe. Add a drizzle of olive oil to the plate and serve with a fresh salad, if you wish.

When the reserved lamb and beans have cooled, refrigerate them until ready to use in the second recipe.

Lamb and Feta Salad

1 leftover cooked lamb steak
   from recipe above
1 roasted red pepper from
   a jar, drained
35g feta, crumbled
100g leftover cooked beans
   from recipe above
2 handfuls of rocket

Dressing
1 tablespoon olive oil
Lemon juice, to taste
Sea salt and freshly ground
   black pepper

Bring the leftover lamb steak and beans to room temperature. Cut the lamb into thin slices. Do the same with the pepper. Mix together the ingredients for the dressing.

Combine the lamb, pepper, feta, beans and rocket. Drizzle over the dressing and serve.

2 FOR 1

BUY 2 LAMB STEAKS, COOK
THEM IN THE FIRST RECIPE
AND USE THE LEFTOVERS IN
THE NEXT RECIPE.

BIG COOK

BUY 2 LAMB SHANKS, COOK THEM IN THE FIRST RECIPE AND USE THE LEFTOVERS IN THE FOLLOWING RECIPES.

Slow-Cooked Lamb Shanks
with olives and polenta

Lamb shank, because it's on the bone, becomes ridiculously tender and tasty when slow-cooked. The sauce here has everything – sweetness, saltiness, richness and piquancy. Two lunches and two dinners from one modest effort seems like a pretty good deal to me! So here we also have Lamb Pitta; Stroganoff and a great sandwich – not bad eh?!

2 lamb shanks (total weight about 750g)
2 tablespoons plain flour, seasoned with salt and pepper
Olive oil, for frying
1 onion, diced
3 garlic cloves, crushed
2 sticks of celery, cut into 1-cm thick slices
150ml red wine
400-g tin of chopped tomatoes
1 teaspoon sugar
1 teaspoon dried oregano
1 tablespoon black olives, pitted
About 60g quick-cook polenta
Knob of butter
Sea salt and freshly ground black pepper

Preheat the oven to 170°C/325°F.

Coat the lamb shanks in the seasoned flour. Heat a little olive oil in a casserole dish over a medium–high heat, then brown the lamb shanks all over for a few minutes. Remove them from the dish and pour away some of the excess fat if it looks like there's a lot.

In the same dish, gently sweat the onion, garlic and celery for 5 minutes. Add the wine and allow to bubble for 2 minutes. Add the tomatoes, sugar and oregano, and season with salt and pepper. Simmer for 5 minutes. Now add the lamb shanks and bring to the boil. Reduce to a simmer and simmer for 1 hour 45 minutes–2 hours until the meat falls off the bone.

Remove the lamb, and shred about three-quarters of the meat off one of the shanks. Keep in a warm place. Put the dish, with the sauce, over a very low heat and add the olives. Simmer gently for 5 minutes. Prepare the polenta according to the packet instructions, then add the butter and plenty of of salt and pepper to taste.

Plate up the polenta, top with the shredded lamb and then spoon over the sauce. Allow the remaining lamb to cool, then cover and refrigerate until ready to use in the next recipes.

Minty Lamb Sandwich

50g leftover cooked lamb shank from
  recipe on page 123
½ tablespoon mayo
1 teaspoon mint sauce
2 slices of bread, or a roll
Small handful of rocket

Cut the lamb into thin pieces. Combine the mayo and mint sauce.
Spread over the bread and layer the lamb and rocket on top.

BIG COOK
LEFTOVERS

Lamb Stroganoff

Olive oil, for frying
1 small onion, diced
¼ teaspoon hot smoked paprika
5 button mushrooms
50g leftover cooked lamb shank from recipe on page 123, torn
1½ tablespoons sour cream
Squeeze of lemon juice
Sea salt and freshly ground black pepper
Pasta or rice, to serve

Heat a little olive oil in a frying pan over a low heat, then add the onion and paprika and sweat the onion for 5 minutes, or until soft but not coloured. Slice the mushrooms and add to the pan. Cook for a further 2–3 minutes. Add the lamb and continue to cook for 2 minutes.

Add the sour cream and cook for a further 2 minutes. Squeeze over a good amount of lemon juice and season to taste with salt and pepper. Serve on pasta or rice.

Lamb, Feta and Hummus Pitta

50g leftover cooked lamb shank from
*   recipe on page 123, torn*
1 pitta bread
Hummus, to serve
35g feta, crumbled
3–4 cherry tomatoes, halved

If you want the leftover lamb warm, reheat it in a frying pan with a little chicken stock over a medium heat. Toast the pitta. Slice to form a pocket (being careful, as they are the hottest things in the world!), spread with hummus and fill with the torn lamb, feta and tomatoes.

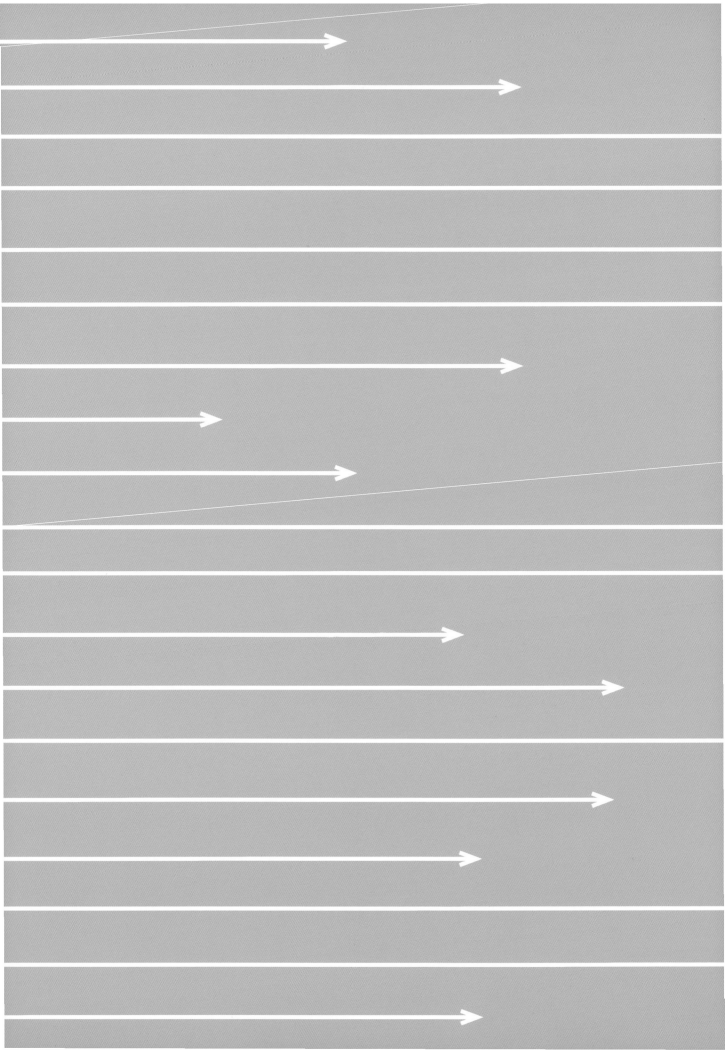

COD AND CHORIZO
WITH PESTO POTATOES AND PEAS

For the first recipe, any firm white fish similar to cod will work a treat. It's a lovely combo of flavours. And the fishcakes take leftovers to such a great place that you'll look for excuses to create leftovers all the time.

500g new potatoes
50g frozen peas
75g chorizo
Olive oil, for frying
2 x 150g cod fillets
2 teaspoons pesto
Sea salt and freshly ground black pepper

Boil the new potatoes in a saucepan of water until tender, about 15 minutes, adding the peas for a minute just before the end of the cooking time.

Meanwhile, skin the chorizo, cut it into quarters and then cut it into ½–1-cm chunks. Rub olive oil all over the cod fillets and season them with salt and pepper.

Heat a little olive oil in a frying pan over a medium heat and fry the chorizo for 2 minutes, or until golden brown. Remove the chorizo from the pan and set aside. In the same pan, cook the cod for 2–3 minutes each side, adding half the chorizo once you have cooked one side, or until the flesh starts to flake easily. If using cod with the skin on, cook it skin side down first.

Once the peas and potatoes are cooked, drain and set half the potatoes aside. To the rest of the potatoes and peas, mix through the pesto.

Plate up by spooning the pesto potatoes and peas in the centre of a plate. Top with one of the fish fillets and surround with the hot chorizo. Add a drizzle more oil, if you wish. Allow the remaining fish fillet, chorizo and potatoes to cool, then cover and refrigerate for the next recipe.

2 FOR 1

BUY 2 COD FILLETS, COOK BOTH IN THE FIRST RECIPE AND USE THE LEFTOVERS IN THE NEXT RECIPE.

CHORIZO FISHCAKES

250g leftover cooked new potatoes from recipe
  on page 130, peeled
1 leftover cooked cod fillet from recipe on page 130
30g leftover fried chorizo from recipe on page 130
Handful of fresh parsley (optional)
2 tablespoons plain flour
1 egg, beaten
Couple of handfuls of breadcrumbs
Olive oil, for frying
Sea salt and freshly ground black pepper

Mash the peeled new potatoes and flake in the cod.

Finely chop the chorizo and parsley, add to the potato mixture and combine. Season with salt and pepper. Shape into 2–3 patties. Dip each one in the flour, then the beaten egg and then the breadcrumbs.

Heat a glug of olive oil in a frying pan over a medium heat, and fry the fishcakes for 5 minutes each side, or until golden, crisp and piping hot.

QUICK PRAWN CURRY

Prawns take centre stage in this pair of recipes. First up, there's a lovely mild, creamy curry with plenty of sauce (some of which could even be kept aside for an instant curry). This is followed by a delightfully crunchy, lemony prawn and green bean salad – a perfect summer plate.

100g raw, shelled prawns
3-cm piece of ginger, peeled
1 garlic clove
1 red onion
1 red chilli
1 tablespoon groundnut oil
¾ tablespoon tikka masala paste
400-ml tin of coconut milk
1 tablespoon tomato purée
Sea salt and freshly ground black
    pepper
Basmati rice, to serve
Fresh coriander, to serve (optional)

Devein the prawns by running a small, sharp knife down the back of them and pulling out the black vein.

Very finely chop the ginger, garlic, onion and chilli either in a food processor, or by hand with a knife. Heat the groundnut oil in a saucepan or frying pan over a low heat, then add the chopped ginger mixture and the tikka masala paste and sweat for 5 minutes. Start preparing your rice at this point.

Add the coconut milk and tomato purée to the curry pan. Simmer for 10 minutes and add salt and pepper to taste. Add the prawns and cook for a couple of minutes until they change colour to pink and they are cooked through. Serve on your rice with coriander, if you wish.

2 FOR 1

BUY 200G RAW PRAWNS AND COOK HALF IN EACH RECIPE.

GRIDDLED PRAWNS WITH LEMONY GREEN BEAN SALAD

100g green beans, topped 'n' tailed
Olive oil, for frying
100g raw, shelled prawns
Little Gem lettuce, torn
1 shallot, thinly sliced
Sea salt and freshly ground black pepper

Dressing
1 teaspoon Dijon mustard
1 tablespoon lemon juice
2 tablespoons crème fraîche
Pinch of sugar

Boil or steam the green beans for a few minutes until they are tender but still have a crunch. Once cooked, run them under cold water to cool and preserve their vibrant colour.

Mix together the ingredients for the dressing.

Devein the prawns by running a small, sharp knife down the back of them and pulling out the black vein. Coat them in olive oil and season with salt and pepper. Put a griddle or frying pan over a high heat and, once smoking hot (make sure your extractor fan is on), add the prawns and cook for 45 seconds each side until they change colour to pink and are cooked.

Chuck together the lettuce, shallot and green beans. Coat in the dressing and top with the griddled prawns.

SEAFOOD PAELLA

Use whatever seafood you can get your hands on to make this paella; I think prawns and mussels work best. You can get handy bags of seafood that are great for no-fuss dinners like this. Leftover paella makes fantastically tasty rice balls – *arancini*. Oven-baking them (rather than deep-frying) keeps them healthier. Fill them with whatever you fancy, for example black olives stuffed with cheese.

Olive oil, for frying
1 onion, diced
1 garlic clove, crushed
50g chorizo, sliced 1cm thick
¼ teaspoon paprika
150g risotto rice
Splash of sherry (optional)
500ml hot chicken stock
Couple of handfuls of your chosen seafood
Sea salt and freshly ground black pepper
Lemon wedge and fresh parsley, to serve

2 FOR 1

MAKE PAELLA RICE IN THE FIRST RECIPE AND USE THE LEFTOVERS IN THE NEXT RECIPE.

Heat 2 tablespoons olive oil in a large frying pan over a low heat and gently sweat the onion and garlic for 5 minutes, or until soft but without colour. Add the chorizo and paprika and cook for 2 minutes.

Add the rice, stirring to coat it in the oils in the pan. Then add a splash of sherry, if using, and cook it until most of it has evaporated. Add the stock, bit by bit, and allow it to be mostly absorbed before adding more. Keep simmering over a gentle heat, stirring, until the stock has been used up and the rice is cooked through, about 15 minutes. Push the chorizo to one side and spoon half the rice into a separate container for the next recipe. Cool it quickly, then refrigerate until ready to use.

At this point, add your chosen seafood to the pan; it's best to cover the pan for this. Timings: cook deveined raw prawns for a couple of minutes until pink; if the prawns are ready-cooked, heat them until warmed through; cook mussels and clams until they are opened and discard any that don't open. Serve with a wedge of lemon and a scattering of parsley.

EASY ARANCINI

175g chilled leftover paella from recipe above
3 cubes of mozzarella or Cheddar, or 3 black olives, to fill (optional)
Plain flour, for dusting
1 egg, beaten
1 slice of bread, processed into breadcrumbs, or 3 tablespoons breadcrumbs

Preheat the oven to 200°C/400°F.

Put some greaseproof paper on a baking tray. (Stick it to the tray with a smear of butter.)

Take the chilled leftover paella, divide it into 3 equal portions and shape them into balls. At this point, you can push a cube of mozzarella or Cheddar, or a black olive, into the centre of the ball and reform the rice around it to cover it. Alternatively, you can leave the arancini plain. Dip each one in the flour, then the beaten egg and then the breadcrumbs.

Roast the arancini on the prepared baking tray in the preheated oven for 20–25 minutes until golden brown and crisp. Serve with a side salad or a quick tomato sauce.

FAST FISH PIE

From start to plate, this fish pie takes 25 minutes max! The breadcrumb crust is a triumph with its blend of lemon, herb and garlic. And it's this crust that packs so much flavour power into your follow-up fishcakes. The quantity of fish needed isn't critical, so a little more will do no harm. If you serve the pie with some boiled new potatoes, make extra and use those leftover potatoes for your fishcakes. Both recipes go well with tomato and shallot salad.

15g butter, plus extra for greasing
2 x 110g white fish fillets (I used haddock)
Juice and grated zest of ½ lemon
50g white, crust-free bread
1 fat garlic clove
2 tablespoons fresh parsley
Drizzle of olive oil
Sea salt and freshly ground black pepper

Preheat the oven to 200°C/400°F.

Grease a baking dish and place the fish fillets inside it. Season it with salt and pepper and drizzle over the lemon juice.

Blitz together the lemon zest, bread, garlic, parsley, butter and oil in a food processor until it forms fine, fragrant breadcrumbs. Scatter this evenly over the fish fillets. Bake, uncovered, in the preheated oven for 15–20 minutes, depending on thickness, until cooked through. Plate up one portion of fast fish pie, with a tomato and shallot salad, green beans or boiled new potatoes. Allow the remaining portion of fish to cool, then cover and refrigerate until ready to use in the next recipe.

10 MINUTE FISHCAKES

Leftover fast fish pie from recipe
  left
250g new potatoes, boiled and
  mashed
2 tablespoons plain flour
1 egg, beaten
Couple of handfuls of
  breadcrumbs
Olive oil, for frying
Sea salt and freshly ground black
  pepper

Flake the leftover fast fish pie (including the topping) and mix it together with the potatoes. Season with salt and pepper. Form into two patties. Dip each one in the flour, then the beaten egg and then the breadcrumbs.

Heat a glug of olive oil in a frying pan over a medium heat, and fry the fishcakes for 5 minutes each side, or until golden, crisp and piping hot.

2 FOR 1

COOK TWO 110G WHITE FISH FILLETS IN THE FIRST RECIPE AND USE THE LEFTOVERS IN THE NEXT RECIPE.

MUSSELS IN BEER

This is a lovely alternative to the classic *moules marinières* using lager instead of wine and giving a darker but sweet flavour. The linguine in the second recipe is a dish I first had at a beach café in Corsica and, even if you've never been there, this great combo of ingredients will transport you there, too. Pure sunshine!

1kg mussels
2 shallots
2 garlic cloves
Knob of butter
1 bottle of light lager (I use Beck's)
1 tablespoon cream
Squeeze of lemon juice
Freshly ground black pepper
Crusty bread or chips, to serve

Wash the mussels thoroughly and 'debeard' them by pulling the hairy 'beards' off the shells. Discard any cracked or open mussels.

Dice the shallots and crush the garlic. Melt the butter in a large saucepan over medium heat, then sweat the shallots and garlic for 5 minutes, or until soft but with no colour. Add the lager and bring to the boil.

Now add the mussels, cover and cook, shaking the pan regularly, for a few minutes until all the mussels have opened.

Remove the mussels with a slotted spoon (keeping the cooking liquor in the pan) and place half in a bowl. Set the remaining mussels aside to cool, then extract them from their shells and refrigerate until ready to use in the next recipe.

Add the cream and lemon juice to the cooking liquor and simmer for a minute or so. Season with black pepper, stir, and pour over the mussels in the bowl. Serve with crusty bread or chips.

2 FOR 1

COOK 1KG MUSSELS IN THE FIRST RECIPE AND USE THE LEFTOVERS IN THE NEXT RECIPE.

MUSSEL LINGUINE

Olive oil, for frying
2 garlic cloves, crushed
400-g tin of chopped
 tomatoes
Pinch of sugar
1 teaspoon chilli flakes
1 teaspoon capers (optional)
100g leftover cooked, shelled
 mussels from recipe above
100g linguine
Sea salt and freshly ground black
 pepper
Fresh parsley, to serve

Put a saucepan of water on for your pasta.

Heat a glug of olive oil in a saucepan over a gentle heat, then sweat the garlic for 2 minutes. Add the tomatoes, sugar, chilli and capers, if using, and simmer very gently for 10–15 minutes. Season with salt and pepper to taste.

Cook the pasta in the pan of boiling water when the time is right.

When the pasta is almost ready, tip the mussels into the tomato sauce and warm through very gently for a minute or two, making sure they don't toughen up. Check the seasoning again.

Plate up your pasta in a large bowl and top with the sauce and a sprinkling of fresh parsley.

SMOKED MACKEREL PATE WITH A KICK

Very healthy, this – and easy; straight out of the packet! All you need is a fork, a bowl and a spoon. The Niçoise that follows has been updated to replace the usual tuna (expensive) with mackerel (sustainable), making something of equal delight…

1 smoked mackerel fillet
1½ tablespoons thick Greek yoghurt
1 teaspoon horseradish sauce
Lemon juice, to taste
Sea salt and freshly ground black
  pepper
Crackers, crisp breads or toast,
  to serve

Peel the skin off the mackerel, then flake the flesh into a bowl. Add the yoghurt and horseradish sauce, and mash and mix with a fork. Add the lemon juice, salt and pepper to taste. Serve chilled on anything crunchy such as crackers, crisp breads or really good toast.

2 FOR 1

BUY 2 SMOKED MACKEREL FILLETS AND USE ONE IN EACH RECIPE.

SMOKED MACKEREL NICOISE

200g new potatoes
40g green beans, topped 'n'
  tailed
1 smoked mackerel fillet
1 tablespoon black olives
3 cherry tomatoes, chopped
Little Gem lettuce, torn
Handful of croutons

Dressing
½ teaspoon sugar
½ teaspoon Dijon mustard
1 tablespoon lemon juice
3 tablespoons extra virgin
  olive oil

Boil the new potatoes in a saucepan of water, adding the green beans when the potatoes are starting to soften. Once everything is cooked, whip out the green beans and run them under cold water to cool and preserve their vibrant colour.

Meanwhile, combine the ingredients for the dressing. Peel the skin off the mackerel, then flake the flesh. Pit the olives.

Put the potatoes, beans, tomatoes, olives and Little Gem in a bowl. Coat in the dressing and top with the flaked mackerel and croutons.

NORDIC SMOKED SALMON WRAP

Smoked salmon is one of those foods that lends itself to quick cooking. The wrap recipe is pure and simple, relying on the high quality of the ingredients; and the pasta in the second recipe is wonderfully creamy, smoky and fresh. Super speedy; maximum effect.

1 tablespoon crème fraîche or cream cheese
1 wrap, such as tortilla wrap
2 slices of smoked salmon (about 30g off-cuts)
1 small avocado, peeled, pitted and sliced
2 cherry tomatoes, chopped
Squeeze of lemon juice
Sea salt and freshly ground black pepper

Spread the crème fraîche or cream cheese over the wrap. Top with the smoked salmon, sliced avocado, chopped tomatoes and lemon juice, and season with salt and pepper. Wrap up, cut in half and enjoy.

2 FOR 1

BUY A SMALL PACK OF SMOKED SALMON AND USE HALF IN EACH RECIPE.

CREAMY SMOKED SALMON PASTA

100g linguine
Handful of peas (optional)
2 tablespoons crème fraîche or cream cheese
1½ tablespoons lemon juice
1 teaspoon fresh dill, torn
2 slices of smoked salmon (about 30g off-cuts)
Sea salt and freshly ground black pepper

Cook your linguine according to the packet instructions. If using peas, stick them in with the pasta 1 minute before it is ready.

Mix together the crème fraîche or cream cheese, lemon juice and dill, and season well with pepper. Chop the salmon into bite-sized pieces.

Once the pasta is cooked, drain it and put it back in the pan with the creamy mixture. Stir well and allow to warm through for a minute. Serve in a large bowl and top with the smoked salmon.

SALMON PARCELS

Due credit to my dad for coming up with the idea of adding the horseradish to these little steamed parcels. It cuts beautifully across the rich oils of the salmon. The subsequent salmon pâté couldn't be easier and makes a great light lunch or snack.

200g new potatoes, scrubbed clean
2 salmon fillets, about 110g each
4 teaspoons horseradish sauce
10 thin slices of peeled cucumber
Knob of butter
1–2 teaspoons torn fresh parsley and/ or dill
Sea salt and freshly ground black pepper

Preheat the oven to 200°C/400°F.

Cut any large new potatoes in half, then boil or steam them for about 15–20 minutes until cooked through.

Meanwhile, place both salmon fillets on a sheet of foil or baking paper in the centre of a baking tray. Season with salt and pepper, then spread the horseradish over them with a knife. Top with the cucumber slices. Pull up the sides of the foil or paper and fold over to seal the salmon in. Cook for 12–15 minutes or until the salmon flakes easily.

Drain the cooked potatoes and toss them with the butter, parsley or dill, and some salt and pepper. Serve with one of the salmon fillets. (This also goes brilliantly with a side salad or green beans.) Allow the other salmon fillet to cool, then refrigerate until ready to use.

SIMPLE SALMON PATE

1 leftover cooked salmon fillet from
  recipe left, skinned
½ tablespoon lemon juice
2 tablespoons crème fraîche or cream
  cheese
Sea salt and freshly ground black
  pepper

Flake the cooked salmon fillet with a fork, then place it in a bowl with the other ingredients. Mash and mix with the fork until well combined. Taste and adjust the seasoning. Serve on hot buttered toast or crackers.

2 FOR 1

BUY 2 SALMON FILLETS, COOK BOTH IN THE FIRST RECIPE AND USE THE LEFTOVERS IN THE NEXT RECIPE.

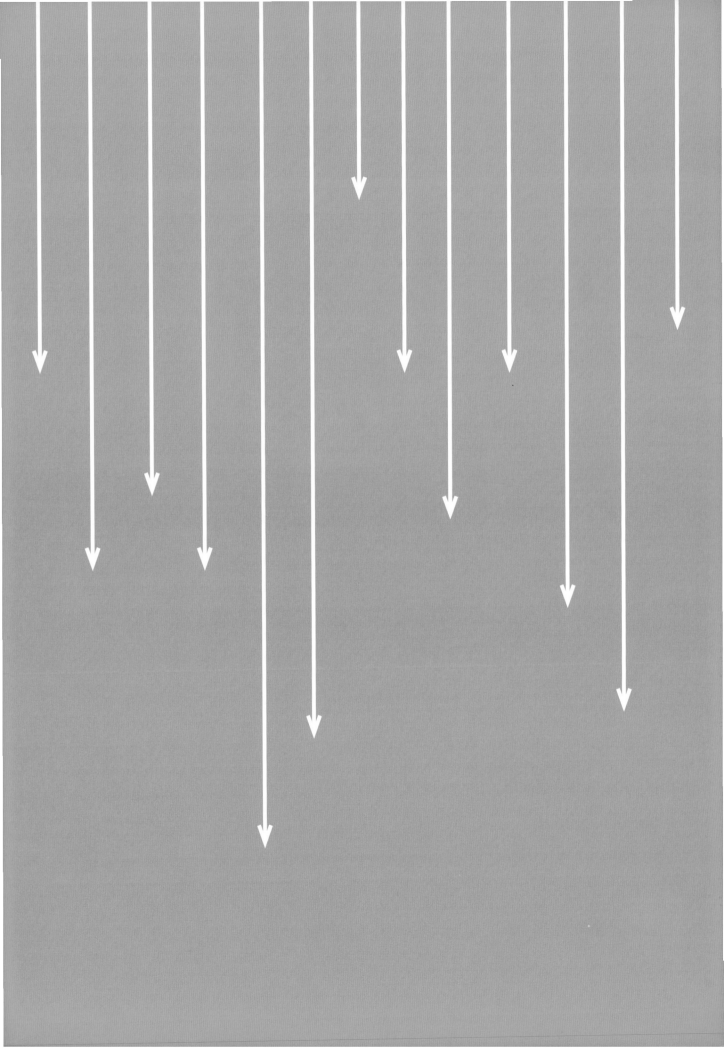

COOK

VEGETABLES

ROAST BUTTERNUT SQUASH
WITH RICOTTA AND ROCKET ON GNOCCHI

You get a lot for your money with a butternut squash. It has a distinctive creamy flavour that works equally well on pasta and gnocchi – as well as making a delightfully addictive dip.

600g butternut squash, peeled and deseeded
1 tablespoon olive oil
2 teaspoons dried thyme
150g gnocchi
1 tablespoon ricotta
Squeeze of lemon juice
Handful of rocket
Sea salt and freshly ground black pepper

Preheat the oven to 200°C/400°F.

Cut the butternut squash into 2-cm cubes. Place into a freezer bag with the olive oil, thyme and some salt and pepper. Seal the bag and shake it to give the squash an even coating and then tip it out of the bag and onto a large baking tray. Cook in the preheated oven for 20 minutes, or until soft and a pale golden colour.

Meanwhile, put a saucepan of water on to boil for the gnocchi, then cook according to the packet instructions. Drain the gnocchi and return to the dry pan with the ricotta and lemon juice, half the cooked butternut squash, and some black pepper. Tip into a bowl and top with rocket and little olive oil. Allow the rest of the butternut squash to cool, cover and refrigerate until ready to use in the next recipe.

2 FOR 1

BUY A BUTTERNUT SQUASH,
COOK IT IN THE FIRST RECIPE
AND USE THE LEFTOVERS IN
THE NEXT RECIPE.

ROAST BUTTERNUT
SQUASH DIP

200g leftover cooked butternut squash from recipe above
100g ricotta
Squeeze of lemon juice
Freshly ground black pepper

Using a food processor or hand blender, blend together the cooked butternut squash, ricotta, lemon juice, and black pepper to taste. Allow to chill in the fridge until ready to use. Serve with crispbreads, hot crusty bread or alongside a deli plate.

CREAMY LEEK AND PEAS
ON WARM CIABATTA

This fancy toast makes a lovely lunch. Bacon is an optional extra, but it does add a complementary dimension to the leek and peas. You can also make this as a side dish for a steak. The Glamorgan sausage recipe nicely uses up any leftover leek and pea mixture. The sausages can be kept in the fridge once shaped, so you can prep them ahead of time if you like. There's even enough for two meals!

300g leek
2 rashers of streaky bacon
   (optional)
Olive oil, for frying
Splash of water
1 ciabatta roll
100g frozen peas
Good squeeze of lemon juice
2 tablespoons crème fraîche
Sea salt and freshly ground black
   pepper

Thinly slice the leek into ½-cm thick rounds. Cut the bacon, if using, into similar-sized pieces. Heat a little olive oil in a saucepan over a medium heat and fry the bacon for 3–4 minutes until the fat begins to run. Add the leek, stir, then add the water. Cover and gently cook for around 10 minutes, stirring occasionally, until the leek is nice and soft.

Meanwhile, cut the ciabatta through the middle, then toast, grill or bake it lightly to warm it. To the leek mixture, add the peas and cook for 1–2 minutes. Remove from the heat, season with salt and pepper to taste, and add the lemon juice. Stir in the crème fraîche. Spoon half of the mixture onto the warm ciabatta and top with a little more black pepper and lemon juice. Allow the remaining leek mixture to cool, then cover and refrigerate it until ready to use in the next recipe.

2 FOR 1

BUY A LEEK AND FROZEN PEAS, COOK THEM IN THE FIRST RECIPE AND USE THE LEFTOVERS IN THE NEXT RECIPE.

LEEK AND PEA
GLAMORGAN SAUSAGES

300g leftover leek mixture from
   recipe above
50g mature Cheddar, grated
1 teaspoon English mustard
100g breadcrumbs

Preheat the oven to 200°C/400°F. Line a baking tray with a sheet of baking paper.

Combine the leek mixture, grated Cheddar, mustard and three-quarters of the breadcrumbs. Shape and squeeze everything into 4 or 5 rough sausage shapes. Put the remaining breadcrumbs on a plate, then dip and roll the sausages in them to get an even coating.

Place the sausages on the prepared baking tray and cook in the preheated oven for 15–20 minutes until golden brown. Allow to sit for a moment and then carefully remove using a spatula. Serve with a tomato salad and a good dollop of apple chutney.

THAI LENTIL DHAL

A variation on the usual Indian dhal, my version is inspired by Thai flavours. It's one of the thriftiest dinners you can make – but it tastes well above its class. The pâté is one of my all-time favourites and also happens to be ridiculously easy to make.

1 tablespoon groundnut oil
2 garlic cloves, crushed
1 onion, diced
3 teaspoons Thai red curry paste
(if you are veggie, check the
packaging, as a lot of pastes include
shrimp or fish sauce)
160g red split lentils, washed
2 teaspoons tomato purée
400-ml tin of coconut milk
100ml water
Juice of ½ lemon
Sea salt and freshly ground black
pepper
Naan bread and chapatis, to serve

Heat the groundnut oil in a large saucepan over a very gentle heat, then sweat the garlic and onion for 5 minutes, or until soft and translucent. Add the curry paste, stir and cook for another minute.

Add the lentils, tomato purée, coconut milk and water. Bring to the boil and simmer for 20 minutes, stirring regularly. Remove from the heat, add the lemon juice, taste and season to taste with salt and pepper.

Plate up half the dhal and serve with naan bread or chapatis, or as an accompaniment to other curries. Allow the other half of the dhal to cool, then refrigerate until ready to use in the following recipe.

2 FOR 1

MAKE A RED-LENTIL DHAL IN THE FIRST RECIPE, THEN USE THE LEFTOVERS IN THE NEXT RECIPE.

LENTIL, COCONUT AND CORIANDER PATE

300g leftover Thai Lentil Dhal
from recipe above
1 large handful of fresh
coriander
Sea salt and freshly ground black
pepper
Lemon juice (optional)
Warm toast or crispbreads,
to serve

Using a food processor or hand blender, blitz the leftover Thai Lentil Dhal with the coriander until you have a nice smooth pâté with specks of green. Taste and season with salt and pepper, and lemon juice if desired.

Allow to chill in the fridge until ready to use. Serve with warm toast or crispbreads.

AUBERGINE AND TOMATO FUSILLI

One aubergine; two dishes! Aubergine has a special place in the kitchen for its unique capacity to absorb flavours – in this case some piquant numbers. This is followed by a salad featuring the deep and earthy taste of miso.

100g aubergine
3 cherry tomatoes
Small handful of fresh basil
100g fusilli
1½ teaspoons red wine vinegar
½ shallot, diced
1 tablespoon olive oil, plus extra
    for frying
Squeeze of lemon juice
Parmesan shavings, to serve
Sea salt and freshly ground black
    pepper

Put a large saucepan of salted water on to boil for the fusilli.

Meanwhile, chop the aubergine into 1½-cm cubes. Cut the tomatoes into quarters. Tear the basil. Combine the red wine vinegar, shallot and the 1 tablespoon olive oil in a bowl.

Cook the pasta according to the packet instructions. Coat the aubergine lightly in olive oil and fry in a frying pan over a medium heat for about 5 minutes until golden and cooked through. Remove from the pan, squeeze over the lemon juice and season with salt and pepper.

Drain the cooked pasta and return it to the pan. Add the aubergine, tomatoes, basil and the vinegar mixture. Combine well and check for seasoning. Plate up, top with Parmesan shavings and squeeze over a little more lemon juice, to taste.

2 FOR 1

BUY ONE AUBERGINE, COOK PART OF IT IN THE FIRST RECIPE AND USE THE REST IN THE NEXT RECIPE.

MISO AUBERGINE SALAD

200g aubergine
1 tablespoon groundnut oil
2 teaspoons brown miso paste
2 teaspoons rice wine
2 teaspoons rice wine vinegar
1 Little Gem lettuce, leaves separated
2 spring onions, finely chopped
Toasted sesame oil, for dressing

Cut the aubergine into 1½-cm wide strips. Toss it in the groundnut oil. Fry it in a saucepan over a medium heat for about 5 minutes or until golden brown.

Meanwhile, combine the miso paste, rice wine and rice wine vinegar in a bowl.

Once the aubergine is soft and well coloured, remove from the heat, add the miso mixture and toss to combine.

Place the leaves in a bowl, top with the aubergine and spring onions, and finally drizzle with sesame oil.

SPICY CHICKPEA AND POTATO SOUP

Here again, cheap ingredients are transformed in the company of harissa, a spice paste widely used in North Africa and the Middle East and which is made from chilli and a mix of over 40 herbs and spices. The Lebanese salad in second place is incredibly healthy and a real doddle!

Olive oil, for frying
1 onion, diced
200g potato, peeled
120g chickpeas (half a 400-g tin, drained)
1–2 teaspoons rose harissa paste (quantity depends on heat required)
500ml vegetable stock
Sea salt and freshly ground black pepper

Heat a glug of olive oil in a saucepan over a gentle heat, then sweat the onion for about 5 minutes, or until translucent. Meanwhile, chop the potato into 1-cm chunks.

Add the potato, drained chickpeas, harissa paste and stock to the pan. Bring to the boil, then simmer for 8–10 minutes or until the potato is soft.

Remove the pan from the heat and blend with a hand blender (or leave to cool slightly and use a blender or food processor) until very smooth. Season to taste.

2 FOR 1

BUY A 400-G TIN OF CHICKPEAS AND USE HALF IN EACH RECIPE.

LEBANESE-STYLE CHICKPEA SALAD

2-cm piece of cucumber
2 cherry tomatoes
1 tablespoon lemon juice
1 tablespoon olive oil
1½ tablespoons each chopped fresh coriander and parsley
120g chickpeas (the remaining half of the 400-g tin, drained)
Sea salt and freshly ground black pepper

Peel and dice the cucumber. Dice the tomatoes. Combine the lemon juice, olive oil and herbs in a bowl. Add the chickpeas, tomatoes and cucumber, combine and season well with salt and pepper.

VEGGIE FAJITAS

You can, of course, play about with the fillings for these fajitas. Peppers, refried beans, onions, courgettes, mushrooms – it's your choice! The Mexican salad is my sister's favourite thing (hardly surprising since it's so good). Be warned; you will want more...

1 aubergine
2 teaspoons rose harissa paste
2 tablespoons olive oil
Squeeze of lemon juice
1–2 tortilla wraps
1–2 tablespoons sour cream or
    crème fraîche
½ avocado, sliced
A little lettuce (optional)
Small handful of fresh coriander
Sea salt and freshly ground black
    pepper

Slice the aubergine into ¼-cm thick rounds or half-rounds. Combine the harissa and olive oil in a bowl and add the aubergine. Stir to coat well. Heat a griddle pan over a high heat until smoking. Quickly season the aubergine with salt and pepper and add it to the hot griddle pan in batches so as not to overcrowd the pan. Cook for 1 minute each side or until nicely charred. Remove to a plate, squeeze over a little lemon juice and cook the remaining aubergine in the same way.

Assemble the fajita: start with the sour cream or crème fraîche, top with half of the aubergine, the avocado, coriander and a little lettuce. Roll up and get stuck in. Allow the leftover aubergine to cool, then cover and refrigerate until ready to use in the next recipe.

2 FOR 1

BUY 1 AUBERGINE AND 1 AVOCADO, USE SOME IN THE FIRST RECIPE, THEN USE THE LEFTOVERS IN THE NEXT RECIPE.

MEXICAN SALAD

Leftover cooked harissa
    aubergine from recipe
    above
Large handful of lightly salted
    tortilla chips
½ avocado, sliced
2 small tomatoes, cut into
    eighths
Small handful of fresh
    coriander
1 Little Gem lettuce, torn
25g Cheddar cheese, grated

Dressing
2 tablespoons olive oil
2 teaspoons balsamic vinegar
1 teaspoon honey
1 teaspoon ketchup
Small pinch of sea salt

Combine the ingredients for the dressing.

In a large bowl, mix the leftover harissa aubergine, the tortilla chips, avocado, tomatoes, coriander, lettuce and grated Cheddar. Top with the dressing and mix with your hands to get an even coating. Tip into a serving dish and you're done!

TOFU AND CUCUMBER SALAD

Tofu is a great receptor of flavour, and this recipe has lots of it. It's a very refreshing, Chinese-inspired dish. The second recipe makes a great, quick starter or can be served with noodles and veg for an exotic main.

1 tablespoon light soy sauce
2 teaspoons toasted sesame oil
225g firm tofu (half a pack), drained and cut into bite-sized chunks
5-cm piece of cucumber, cut lengthways into ribbons with a mandoline or vegetable peeler
1 spring onion, shredded
Small handful of fresh coriander, torn

Combine the soy sauce and sesame oil in a bowl. Pat the tofu dry with kitchen paper.

Put the cucumber in a shallow bowl and top with the tofu, spring onion and coriander. Drizzle with the soy sauce dressing.

2 FOR 1

BUY A 450-G PACK OF FIRM TOFU AND USE HALF IN EACH RECIPE.

SALT 'N' PEPPER TOFU

225g firm tofu (half a pack), drained and cut into bite-sized chunks
½ teaspoon coarse sea salt
½ teaspoon sugar
¾ teaspoon whole Szechuan peppercorns
½ tablespoon plain flour
1 teaspoon toasted sesame oil
1 shallot, very thinly sliced
Groundnut oil, for frying
Egg noodles, to serve

Pat the tofu dry with kitchen paper. Crush the sea salt, sugar and Szechuan peppercorns with a pestle and mortar or a spice grinder until it becomes a fine powder. Mix the powder with the flour. Dip the tofu chunks in this powder until evenly coated.

Heat a good glug of oil in a frying pan over a medium–high heat. Fry the tofu for about 1 minute each side, or until golden brown. Meanwhile, heat the sesame oil in a separate pan and fry the shallot until crispy.

Serve the tofu and shallot with egg noodles.

GRIDDLED SPRING ONION TART

This lovely duo of thrifty Mediterranean tarts makes use of quick and easy ready-made puff pastry. The fresh flavours here make for a delightful light lunch or supper – and served with a salad, you can easily get a couple of portions out of each.

6 spring onions
Olive oil, for frying
160g all-butter puff pastry
  (half a 320-g pack)
75g feta, crumbled
½–1 tablespoon chopped fresh mint
Freshly ground black pepper

Preheat the oven to 220°C/425°F.

Heat a griddle pan over a high heat until smoking (make sure your extractor fan is on). Top and tail the spring onions and coat with a little olive oil. Put the spring onions on the hot griddle pan to cook for 2 minutes each side, or until they have a nice char. Remove the pan from the heat and set the onions aside.

Using a rolling pin, roll out the puff pastry on a lightly floured board to a rectangle about 3–4mm thick. Place on a baking tray and top with the crumbled feta. Arrange the spring onions on top, scatter over the mint and season well with pepper. Add a final drizzle of olive oil if you wish.

Bake in the preheated oven for 10–12 minutes or until golden brown, puffed up and cooked through. Serve with a side salad.

2 FOR 1

BUY A 320-G PACK OF PUFF PASTRY AND USE HALF IN EACH RECIPE.

ARTICHOKE HEART, BASIL AND MOZZARELLA TART

75g mozzarella
100g artichoke hearts in a jar, drained of oil
160g all-butter puff pastry (half a 320-g pack)
1 tablespoon fresh basil leaves, torn
Sea salt and freshly ground black pepper
Olive oil, for frying

Preheat the oven to 220 °C/425 °F.

Thinly slice the mozzarella and roughly chop the drained artichoke hearts.

Using a rolling pin, roll out the puff pastry on a lightly floured board to a rectangle about 3–4mm thick. Place on a baking tray and top evenly with the mozzarella, then add the artichoke hearts, basil, salt and pepper and a drizzle of olive oil.

Bake in the preheated oven for 10–12 minutes or until golden brown, puffed up and cooked through. Finish with a little more basil and serve with a tomato and red onion salad.

RATATOUILLE

In this tasty duo of recipes, strong ingredients combine to make wonderfully rich flavours. I particularly like the piquancy from the capers and olives. Everything works really well when transformed into the soup, served minestrone-style. Bellissimo!

1 aubergine
1 courgette
Olive oil, for frying
1 small onion, diced
400-g tin of chopped tomatoes
½ tablespoon balsamic vinegar
1 teaspoon capers
½ tablespoon black olives, pitted
2 pinches of dried thyme
Sea salt and freshly ground black
    pepper

Cut the aubergine and courgette into quarters, lengthways, then cut into bite-sized chunks. Stick these into a bowl and drizzle with olive oil and a little salt and pepper. Mix well until they have an even coating.

Put a frying pan over a high heat and cook the aubergine and courgette for 3–4 minutes until golden brown. You may want to cook them in batches to avoid overcrowding the pan. Remove to a plate and set aside.

Heat a glug of olive oil in the same pan over a gentle heat and sweat the onion for about 5 minutes until soft and translucent. Add the tomatoes, balsamic vinegar, capers, olives and thyme and simmer gently for about 5 minutes.

Add the aubergine and courgette, cover and simmer gently for about 10 minutes or until soft. Taste and adjust the seasoning; remember that the olives and capers provide salty bursts, so you might not need to add much.

Plate up half the ratatouille and serve with lovely crusty bread or as a side dish to a roast or any bits you fancy. It also makes a cracking filling for a sandwich, hot or cold. Keep the other half for the next recipe, which you can start straightaway or allow to cool, then cover and refrigerate.

2 FOR 1

MAKE A BIG PORTION OF RATATOUILLE IN THE FIRST RECIPE AND USE THE LEFTOVERS IN THE NEXT RECIPE.

RATATOUILLE AND PASTA SOUP

50g macaroni pasta
300g leftover ratatouille from recipe on page 166
About 200ml vegetable stock
Olive oil, for drizzling

Put a saucepan of salted water on to boil for the pasta. Cook according to the packet instructions, then drain.

Meanwhile, blend half the leftover ratatouille mix in a blender or food processor until smooth. Tip into a saucepan with the vegetable stock and the remaining ratatouille. Add a little more stock if you like a thinner soup. Heat, stirring occasionally, until piping hot. Add the pasta just before serving, and drizzle a little olive oil on top.

PASTA WITH ROASTED PEPPERS AND GOAT'S CHEESE

Roasted peppers from a jar are fantastic and they take out all the fuss and faff so you can create these delicious dishes in no time. The pasta dish is rich, creamy but fresh, and the Turkish pizza is based on a clever, foolproof dough that provides a lovely contrast to this gorgeous topping.

100g pasta of your choice
Olive oil, for frying
1 small onion, diced
1 garlic clove, crushed
50g roasted red peppers from a jar, drained
25g goat's cheese
Squeeze of lemon juice
Sea salt and freshly ground black pepper

Put a saucepan of cold water, with a dash of salt, on to boil for the pasta. Cook the pasta according to the packet instructions to coincide with the timings for the sauce.

Heat a glug of olive oil in a saucepan over a gentle heat, then sweat the onion and garlic for 5 minutes, or until soft and translucent. Roughly chop the roasted red peppers, add to the pan and cook for a further 1–2 minutes.

Blitz the contents of the pan with a hand blender, or transfer to a food processor and blitz until smooth. Add the goat's cheese and blitz again until smooth. Season with salt and pepper to taste.

Once the pasta has cooked, drain and then fold in the sauce. Finish with a squeeze of lemon juice and more black pepper.

2 FOR 1

BUY A JAR OF ROASTED RED PEPPERS AND USE SOME IN EACH RECIPE.

FAST TURKISH PIZZA

75g plain flour, sifted
60ml natural yoghurt
Handful of finely chopped fresh basil
Pinch of sea salt

Topping
Olive oil
Handful of roasted red peppers from a jar, drained and sliced
Handful of crumbled goat's cheese
A few thin slices of red onion

Other optional toppings
Tomato, olives, feta, pine nuts, artichoke hearts, coriander, parsley
   or any antipasti you can think of!

Preheat the grill.

Combine the flour, yoghurt, basil and salt in a large bowl. Mix with your
hands until it comes together into a dough. Divide into 2 balls and, using a
rolling pin, roll each into very thin circles on a floured board.

Heat a dry frying pan until hot, then add one dough base and cook for 1–2
minutes each side until browned. Repeat with the other base. Drizzle each
with a little olive oil. Top with the red peppers, goat's cheese, red onion
and a little more oil. Stick under the grill for a few minutes until the cheese
has melted and starts to brown, but watch that the dough doesn't burn.

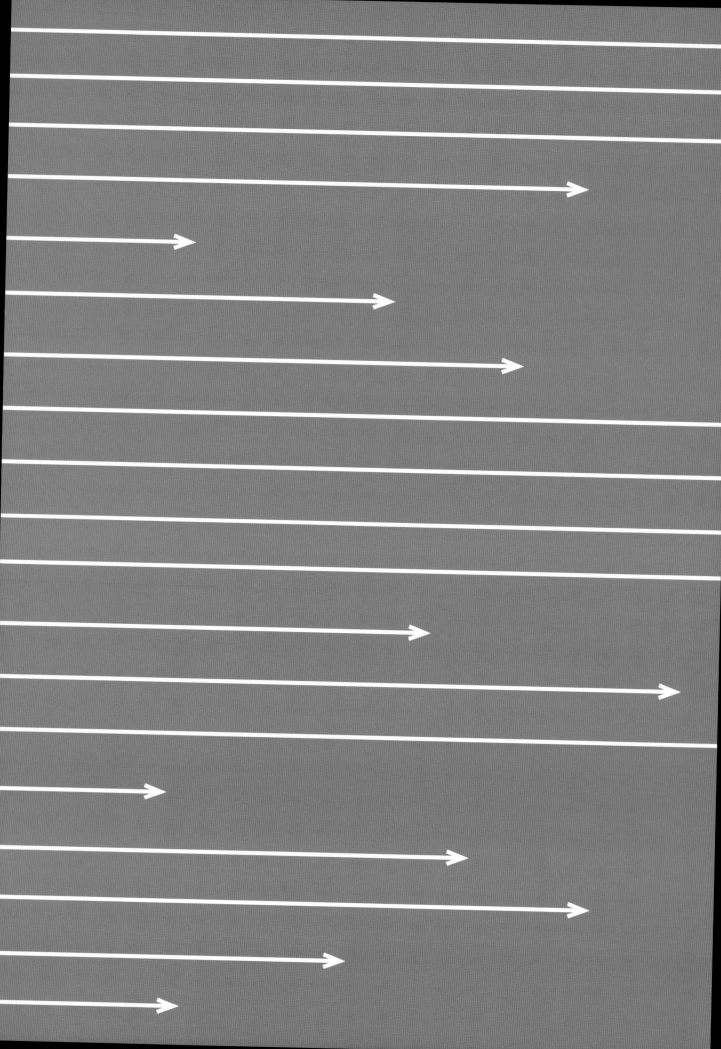

SWEET

TREATS

POPCORN

Popcorn can actually be very healthy – if you avoid adding sugary toppings! These are my versions of the going-to-the-cinema classics of sweet and salty. Not especially healthy, but great fun to make and eat, and wonderfully moreish and indulgent.

25g popcorn kernels
Groundnut oil

Add enough groundnut oil to coat the bottom of a large, heavy-bottomed saucepan. Place over a medium–high heat and add the popcorn. Cover with a lid and cook, shaking the pan regularly, until the popping stops!

STICKY TOFFEE

15g brown sugar
15g butter
2 teaspoons golden syrup

Make a batch of popcorn following the instructions above.

Mix the sugar, butter and golden syrup together in a saucepan and melt over a gentle heat. Boil gently for 1–2 minutes, then pour over the hot popcorn.

PECORINO

15g butter, melted
10g pecorino cheese, finely grated

Make a batch of popcorn following the instructions above.

Toss the hot popcorn in the melted butter, then stir in the grated pecorino cheese.

A BOWL OF POPCORN IN FRONT OF A MOVIE IS A MUST! IT'S SO EASY TO MAKE AND YOU CAN PLAY AROUND WITH SWEET AND SAVOURY FLAVOURS.

COOKIE ROLLS

Yes – instant cookies! Keep the dough in the fridge for a week or more (or even longer in the freezer), and cut off and bake a slice whenever you yearn for that freshly baked biccie.

225g salted butter, softened
200g soft brown sugar
100g caster sugar
1 teaspoon vanilla extract
2 large eggs, beaten
175g plain flour
1 level teaspoon bicarbonate
    of soda
1 teaspoon salt
125g milk chocolate, finely chopped,
    or chocolate chips
75g raisins
200g rolled oats (porridge oats)

Cream together the butter and both sugars in a mixing bowl using a wooden spoon or electric beater until the mixture becomes light and fluffy. Add the vanilla extract and then gradually add the eggs, beating until well combined.

Fold in the flour, bicarbonate of soda and salt until combined, then fold in the chocolate, raisins and oats. Once everything has come together into a dough, spoon it into a rough log shape on a double thickness of baking paper. Roll this up to make a long roll with the diameter of an average cookie – about 5–8cm. Twist the ends of the paper to roughly seal. The exact shape can be adjusted before cooking so don't worry too much. Put on a plate and refrigerate for at least 1 hour.

Preheat the oven to 180°C/350°F.

Slice off 1-cm thick rounds (however many you want in one sitting!), cutting through the baking paper. Reshape the discs if they are a little squashed. Place on a greased baking tray and bake in the preheated oven for 10 minutes, or until golden. Allow to sit on the tray for a few moments, then transfer to a wire rack using a spatula and allow to cool for a few minutes.

Keep the remaining log of cookie dough in the fridge or freezer until next time!

APPLE OAT CRUMBLE

This is a lovely adaptation of the traditional baked apple; here all the ingredients are cooked inside it, so they combine to create something really special.

15g rolled oats (porridge oats)
10g butter
10g caster sugar
½ teaspoon ground cinnamon
1 medium cooking apple

Preheat the oven to 180 ° C/350 ° F.

Roughly combine the oats, butter, sugar and cinnamon in a bowl.

To prepare the apple, using a sharp knife at a 45-degree angle, cut 1.5cm from the stalk, around the centre, to remove the core and a little of the top. You should end up removing a triangular shape. Then use a teaspoon to remove any remaining core, being careful to keep the base intact.

Lightly score a line around the apple, about one-third down, and score twice from this line to the hole at the top. This will help the apple keep its shape while it bakes.

Stuff the cavity with the oat mixture and bake on a tray in the preheated oven for 20–25 minutes or until the apple is soft but not collapsed, and the topping is crunchy. Remove and serve with a little ice cream or even a little custard.

YOU'LL HAVE MOST OF THESE INGREDIENTS IN YOUR STORECUPBOARD ALREADY, SO YOU JUST NEED TO BUY A COOKING APPLE.

INSTANT CHEESECAKE

This is simply a quick assembly job that can include your favourite soft fruit. Just make sure you have enough of the fruit for a good topping, too. This is the kind of recipe that's needed for those special times when you want to be really self-indulgent.

2 digestive biscuits
15g cold, salted butter
25g strawberries, plus extra, halved, for topping (or any other soft fruit)
15g icing sugar
125g cold cream cheese (I use the light version), or cold mascarpone

Put the biscuits in a freezer bag, seal and then bash them with a rolling pin or similar to crush them into crumbs. Pour the crumbs into a bowl, add the butter and rub together to combine them roughly. Spoon them into a ramekin or glass and pat down and compress.

Using a hand blender (or just a fork), blitz together the strawberries and sugar. Combine with the cream cheese and spoon on top of the biscuit base in the ramekin. Cover the top with the extra, halved strawberries. Eat immediately or allow to chill in the fridge or freezer for about 20 minutes for a slightly firmer texture.

YOU CAN SWAP PRETTY
MUCH ANY FRUIT FOR
STRAWBERRIES HERE.
BERRIES AND SOFT FRUITS
WORK PARTICULARLY WELL.

FROZEN CUPCAKES

Make 6 of these cupcakes, freeze them and have one treat weekly – heaven. They're simply delicious and a lifesaver when you come home craving a sweet treat but have no energy to spare!

90g self-raising flour
Small pinch of baking powder
90g salted butter, softened
90g caster sugar
1½ large eggs (or 2 medium),
*   at room temperature*
½ teaspoon vanilla extract

Preheat the oven to 180˚C/350˚F. Line a muffin or cupcake tin with 6 cupcake cases.

Sift the flour and baking powder into a mixing bowl. Tip the butter and sugar into a second, larger mixing bowl. Beat with a wooden spoon (or an electric beater) for 4 minutes or until pale, creamy and light.

Beat the eggs with a fork, then add a dribble at a time to the butter mixture, beating as you go. Don't worry if it splits, just add a little of the flour and mix to bring it back together. Add the vanilla extract.

Add the sifted flour mixture and fold in with a large metal spoon until just mixed. Spoon an equal amount into each cupcake case using 2 spoons, but don't press it down.

Bake in the preheated oven for 15–20 minutes until golden and springy to the touch. Close the oven door very slowly if not quite done so they don't collapse. Remove from the oven, take the cupcakes out of the tin and allow to cool on a rack. Once cooled, you can freeze these for a month or so, in an airtight container. When required, remove from the freezer and allow to come to room temperature over a few hours. Top with one of the icings below.

ICINGS

Mascarpone, honey and stem ginger icing (per cupcake)

1 tablespoon mascarpone
1 teaspoon honey
1 small piece of crystallised
*   stem ginger*

Combine the mascarpone and honey and pipe or spoon onto a cupcake. Thinly slice the stem ginger and pop on top of the icing.

Lime meringue (for 4 cupcakes)

1 large egg white
50g caster sugar
3 teaspoons lime juice
A little grated lime zest

Using a balloon whisk or electric beater, whisk the egg white until it forms soft peaks. Gradually add the sugar and continue to whisk until it forms hard peaks. Now quickly whisk in the lime juice. Pipe or spoon onto the cupcakes and then blowtorch or stick under a hot grill until golden. Top with the grated lime zest.

You can leave out the lime, if you like, to make an unflavoured meringue, but spread some lemon curd over the cupcake before you top it with the plain meringue.

BREAD AND MAPLE SYRUP PUDDING

What to do with slices of leftover bread? Turn them into the ultimate in sweet comfort food – bread-and-butter pudding! Even if you choose to use packet or tinned custard this is a winner and the maple syrup makes it irresistible. And it's dead easy…

Butter
1–2 slices of bread
Handful of raisins
100ml custard
3 teaspoons maple syrup

Preheat the oven to 180°C/350°F.

Grease a small ovenproof dish. Generously butter the slices of bread and cut the crusts off if you wish. Cut into 1.5-cm 'soldiers' or small triangles.

Arrange enough bread in the bottom of the dish to cover it, then sprinkle over the raisins. Pour over the custard and then layer with the leftover bread. Drizzle over the maple syrup. Bake in the preheated oven for 20 minutes, or until piping hot and the bread is crisp and golden.

WE HAVE TWO RECIPES HERE THAT MAKE BRILLIANT USE OF THE SLICED BREAD YOU MIGHT BE STRUGGLING TO GET THROUGH IN THE WEEK.

CINNAMON TOAST

My childhood is filled with food memories, not least this treat, which we used to have in Betty's famous tea rooms in York. Sticky, buttery, crunchy and with that superb cinnamon spice: dangerously good.

25g butter, softened
20g caster sugar
½ teaspoon ground cinnamon
A few drops of vanilla extract
   (optional)
2 slices of bread (brown or white)

Preheat the grill.

Combine the butter, sugar, cinnamon and vanilla extract.

Lightly toast one side of the bread under the grill. Once done, spread the untoasted side with the butter mixture, right up to the edges. Stick back under the grill for about 1 minute, making sure the sugar/toast doesn't burn. Remove, slice into 'soldiers' and enjoy.

MICROWAVEABLE MUG CAKES

Who wouldn't say yes to a lovely gooey cake that cooks in a couple of minutes? Especially when there's hardly any washing up to do! This is the perfect dessert for a sweet-tooth, solo indulgence! Eat straight from the mug (or grease the sides beforehand if you want to turn it out).

NUTELLA

3 tablespoons self-raising flour
3 tablespoons Nutella
1 large egg
2 tablespoons milk
1 tablespoon groundnut or other flavourless oil

Mix all the ingredients in a very large coffee mug (or if you don't have one, divide into 2 smaller mugs, once mixed).

Microwave for between 1 minute 30 seconds and 2 minutes, depending on the strength of your microwave. I found it was just right at 1 minute 45 seconds using my 900W microwave. It should still be a little gooey on top and throughout. Serve with a scoop of vanilla ice cream.

STICKY TOFFEE

25g dates, stoned
1 decent pinch of bicarbonate of soda
2 tablespoons boiling water
30g light brown sugar
20g salted butter, softened
½ large egg, beaten
35g self-raising flour

Toffee sauce
15g brown sugar
15g butter
2 teaspoons golden syrup
Dash of cream (optional)

Chop the dates into small pieces. Combine with the bicarbonate of soda and boiling water, then set aside.

Cream together the sugar and butter in a bowl with a wooden spoon until light and fluffy. Add the egg and mix. It will split at this point but beating in a large pinch of flour will bring it back together. Fold in the rest of the flour with a large metal spoon, then fold in the date mixture. Spoon the mixture into a medium-sized mug.

Microwave for 3 minutes 30 seconds at 600W, or until a metal skewer comes out clean when inserted in the middle of the pudding.

Meanwhile, make the toffee sauce by combining the ingredients in a saucepan, melting over a gentle heat and boiling for a minute or two. Finally, add the cream, if you wish.

I like to prick the pudding all over with a skewer, once cooked, and then pour over the sauce. Allow to sit for a minute because it (and the mug) will be REALLY hot.

CAKE FOR ONE? YES PLEASE! CHOOSE FROM TWO FLAVOURS AND TRY THEM WHEN YOU NEED A SWEET HIT.

INDEX

A

apples: apple oat crumble 177
  chops, chorizo and cheese 89
  pork, apple and sage potato cakes
    102
  quick apple sauce 89
  roast belly pork 100–1
arancini 136
artichoke heart, basil and
  mozzarella tart 164
Asian chicken salad 14
Asian slaw 62
asparagus: smokey duck breast
  with griddled asparagus 46
aubergines: aubergine and tomato
  fusilli 152
  aubergine chicken parmigiana 33
  Mexican salad 157
  miso aubergine salad 154
  rack of lamb with couscous and
    griddled aubergine 108
  ratatouille 166
  veggie fajitas 157
avocados: Nordic smoked salmon
  143
  teriyaki nachos 17

B

baked beans: quick cassoulet 98
BBQ beef rib sandwich 67
BBQ beef ribs 67
BBQ chicken burger 28
BBQ duck rolls with hot sauce 53
beans 9
  chipotle steak and cheese
    quesadillas 66
  lamb and feta salad 120
  lamb steaks with rosemary
    cannellini beans 120
  quick cassoulet 98
beef 10
  BBQ beef rib sandwich 67
  BBQ beef ribs 67
  beef and ale pie 58
  bubble and squeak cakes 60
  chipotle steak and cheese
    quesadillas 66
  cottage pie 73
  ginger beef burger with Asian
    slaw 62
  hot beef sandwich 78
  miso steak and chilli sweet potato
    66

Philly cheesesteak sandwich 56
pho 80
posh mince and tatties 72
roast beef 74–5
spag bol 76
spaghetti and meatballs 64
spicy stir-fried beef 68
steak and roasted red pepper
  salad 57
beer: beef and ale pie 58
  beer and orange chicken 14
  mussels in beer 140
beetroot: beetroot and lamb 114
  lamb and mint burger 114
black fungus, sweet chilli pork stir
  fry with 86
bread: BBQ duck rolls with hot
  sauce 53
  bread and maple syrup pudding
    182
  cinnamon toast 183
  creamy leek and peas on warm
    ciabatta 150
  fast fish pie 138
  horseradish toasts 57
  minty lamb sandwich 124
  shepherd's pie 110
  see also sandwiches
breakfast hash 92
broad beans: warm lamb salad 108
broccoli: egg fried rice with garlic
  broccoli 70
bubble and squeak cakes 60
burgers: BBQ chicken burger 28
  ginger beef burger with Asian
    slaw 62
  lamb and mint burger 114
butternut squash: roast butternut
  squash dip 148
  roast butternut squash with
    ricotta and rocket on gnocchi
    148

C

cabbage: Asian slaw 62
  bubble and squeak cakes 60
cakes: frozen cupcakes 180
  Nutella mug cakes 184
  sticky toffee mug cakes 184
cannellini beans: lamb and feta
  salad 120
  lamb steaks with rosemary
    cannellini beans 120
caramel: sticky toffee mug cakes
  184
  sticky toffee popcorn 174
carrots: Asian slaw 62

cassoulet, quick 98
cheese: artichoke heart, basil and
  mozzarella tart 164
  aubergine chicken parmigiana 33
  chipotle steak and cheese
    quesadillas 66
  chorizo, feta and roasted red
    pepper omelette 91
  chops, chorizo and cheese 89
  creamy pasta frittata 26
  duck, feta and spinach filo pie 50
  easy arancini 136
  fast Turkish pizza 171
  griddled spring onion tart 162
  lamb and feta salad 120
  lamb, feta and hummus pitta
    127
  leek and pea Glamorgan sausages
    150
  pasta with roasted peppers and
    goat's cheese 170
  pecorino popcorn 174
  Philly cheesesteak sandwich 56
  roast butternut squash dip 148
  roast butternut squash with
    ricotta and rocket on gnocchi
    148
cheesecake 178
chicken 10
  Asian chicken salad 14
  aubergine chicken parmigiana 33
  baked lemon chicken legs 32
  BBQ chicken burger 28
  beer and orange chicken 14
  chicken and chorizo pasta bowl
    30
  chicken and leek pasta 24
  chicken and tarragon potato cake
    37
  chicken saag curry 18
  chicken sandwiches 36
  chicken soup 38
  chicken teriyaki 16
  chicken tikka kebabs 20
  flattened griddled chicken with
    cous cous 22
  Moroccan salad 22
  roast chicken 34–5
  teriyaki nachos 17
chicken livers: chicken liver wrap 23
  liver pâté 23
chickpeas: chickpea and potato
  soup, spicy 156
  Lebanese style chickpea salad 156
chilli: chilli sweet potato wedges 28
  five-spice duck legs with chilli
    sweet potato mash 42

miso steak and chilli sweet potato 66

spicy stir-fried beef 68

sweet chilli pork stir fry with black fungus 86

Chinese slow-cooked pork 88

chipotle steak and cheese quesadillas 66

chocolate: cookie rolls 176

Nutella mug cakes 184

ultimate chocolate milkshake 28

chorizo: chicken and chorizo pasta bowl 30

chops, chorizo and cheese 89

chorizo and sweet potato soup 90

chorizo, feta and roasted red pepper omelette 91

chorizo fishcakes 132

cod and chorizo with pesto potatoes and peas 130

quick cassoulet 98

cinnamon toast 183

cod: chorizo fishcakes 132

cod and chorizo with pesto potatoes and peas 130

cookie rolls 176

coriander: harissa pork with mango and coriander couscous 84

lentil, coconut and coriander pâté 151

cottage pie 73

couscous: flattened griddled chicken with cous cous 22

harissa pork with mango and coriander couscous 84

Moroccan salad 22

rack of lamb with couscous and griddled aubergine 108

cream cheese: cheesecake 178

liver pâté 23

Philly cheesesteak sandwich 56

crumble, apple oat 177

cucumber: tofu and cucumber salad 158

cupcakes, frozen 180

curry: chicken liver wrap 23

chicken saag curry 18

quick prawn curry 134

Thai lentil dhal 151

custard: bread and maple syrup pudding 182

D

dhal, Thai lentil 151

dip, roast butternut squash 148

duck: BBQ duck rolls with hot sauce 53

duck, feta and spinach filo pie 50

duck legs in plum sauce with Asian greens 44

duck ragu 45

five-spice duck legs with chilli sweet potato mash 42

lettuce wraps with shredded duck and hoisin sauce 42

roast duck 48–9

smokey duck breast with griddled asparagus 46

Vietnamese duck salad 47

E

eggs: chorizo, feta and roasted red pepper omelette 91

creamy pasta frittata 26

egg fried rice with garlic broccoli 70

spaghetti carbonara 94

F

fajitas, veggie 157

filo pie: duck, feta and spinach 50

fish 11

fast fish pie 138

see also cod, salmon etc

fishcakes: chorizo fishcakes 132

10 minute fish cakes 139

five-spice duck legs with chilli sweet potato mash 42

frankfurters: pork and split pea soup 104

frittata, creamy pasta 26

fusilli, aubergine and tomato 152

G

gammon: maple-glazed gammon steak 94

spaghetti carbonara 94

garlic and lemon chops 115

ginger: ginger beef burger with Asian slaw 62

mascarpone, honey and stem ginger icing 180

Glamorgan sausages, leek and pea 150

gnocchi: roast butternut squash with ricotta and rocket on gnocchi 148

goat's cheese: pasta with roasted peppers and goat's cheese 170

green beans: griddled prawns with lemony green bean salad 135

H

haddock: fast fish pie 138

harissa: chickpea and potato soup, spicy 156

harissa pork with mango and coriander couscous 84

herbs 8

hoisin sauce, lettuce wraps with shredded duck and 42

horseradish: horseradish toasts 57

salmon parcels 144

smoked mackerel pâté with a kick 142

hummus: lamb, feta and hummus pitta 127

I

ice cream: ultimate chocolate milkshake 28

icings 180

K

kebabs, chicken tikka 20

kofta wrap 112

L

lamb 10–11

beetroot and lamb 114

garlic and lemon chops 115

kofta wrap 112

lamb and feta salad 120

lamb and mint burger 114

lamb, feta and hummus pitta 127

lamb potato cakes 118

lamb steaks with rosemary cannellini beans 120

lamb stir-fry 115

lamb stroganoff 125

minty lamb sandwich 124

one-pot lamb stew 116

rack of lamb with couscous and griddled aubergine 108

shepherd's pie 110

slow-cooked lamb shanks with olives and polenta 123

spring broth with lamb 117

tikka lamb chops 118

warm lamb salad 108

Lebanese style chickpea salad 156

leeks: chicken and leek pasta 24

creamy leek and peas on warm ciabatta 150

leek and pea Glamorgan sausages 150

lemon: baked lemon chicken legs 32
  garlic and lemon chops 115
lentils: lentil, coconut and coriander pâté 151
  sausage and lentil stew 93
  Thai lentil dhal 151
lettuce wraps with shredded duck and hoisin sauce 42
lime meringue 180
linguine: creamy smoked salmon pasta 143
  mussel linguine 140
liver *see* chicken livers

M

macaroni: chicken soup 38
  ratatouille and pasta soup 168
mackerel *see* smoked mackerel
mangoes: harissa pork with mango and coriander couscous 84
  Vietnamese duck salad 47
maple syrup: bread and maple syrup pudding 182
  maple-glazed gammon steak 94
mascarpone, honey and stem ginger icing 180
meatballs: sausage meatballs and pasta 96
  spaghetti and meatballs 64
meringue, lime 180
Mexican salad 157
milkshake, ultimate chocolate 28
minty lamb sandwich 124
miso aubergine salad 154
miso steak and chilli sweet potato 66
Moroccan salad 22
mushrooms: beef and ale pie 58
  beer and orange chicken 14
  breakfast hash 92
  lamb stroganoff 125
  sweet chilli pork stir fry with black fungus 86
mussels: mussel linguine 140
  mussels in beer 140
mustard 9

N

nachos, teriyaki 17
noodles: pho 80
Nordic smoked salmon 143
Nutella mug cakes 184

O

oats: apple oat crumble 177
  cookie rolls 176

oils 8
olives: slow-cooked lamb shanks with olives and polenta 123
omelette: chorizo, feta and roasted red pepper 91
one-pot lamb stew 116
onions, spiced 118
orange: beer and orange chicken 14
  Moroccan salad 22

P

paella, seafood 136
pak choi: duck legs in plum sauce with Asian greens 44
pasta: aubergine and tomato fusilli 152
  chicken and chorizo pasta bowl 30
  chicken and leek pasta 24
  chicken soup 38
  creamy pasta frittata 26
  creamy smoked salmon pasta 143
  duck ragu 45
  mussel linguine 140
  pasta with roasted peppers and goat's cheese 170
  ratatouille and pasta soup 168
  sausage and mustard pasta 93
  sausage meatballs and pasta 96
  spag bol 76
  spaghetti and meatballs 64
  spaghetti carbonara 94
pâtés: lentil, coconut and coriander pâté 151
  liver pâté 23
  simple salmon pâté 145
peas: creamy leek and peas on warm ciabatta 150
  leek and pea Glamorgan sausages 150
peas, split: pork and split pea soup 104
pecorino popcorn 174
peppers: chorizo, feta and roasted red pepper omelette 91
  fast Turkish pizza 171
  lamb and feta salad 120
  pasta with roasted peppers and goat's cheese 170
  steak and roasted red pepper salad 57
pesto: cod and chorizo with pesto potatoes and peas 130
Philly cheesesteak sandwich 56
pho 80
pickles 16
pies: beef and ale pie 58

cottage pie 73
duck, feta and spinach filo pie 50
fast fish pie 138
shepherd's pie 110
pitta, lamb, feta and hummus 127
pizza, fast Turkish 171
plum sauce, duck legs in 44
polenta, slow-cooked lamb shanks with olives and 123
popcorn 174
pork 10
  belly pork salad with spicy sesame dressing 88
  Chinese slow-cooked pork 88
  chops, chorizo and cheese 89
  harissa pork with mango and coriander couscous 84
  pork and split pea soup 104
  pork, apple and sage potato cakes 102
  pork sandwich with quick apple sauce 89
  roast belly pork 100–1
  satay pork sandwich 103
  sweet chilli pork stir fry with black fungus 86
posh mince and tatties 72
potatoes: baked lemon chicken legs 32
  breakfast hash 92
  bubble and squeak cakes 60
  chicken and tarragon potato cake 37
  chickpea and potato soup, spicy 156
  chorizo fishcakes 132
  cod and chorizo with pesto potatoes and peas 130
  cottage pie 73
  lamb potato cakes 118
  maple-glazed gammon steak 94
  one-pot lamb stew 116
  pork, apple and sage potato cakes 102
  posh mince and tatties 72
  roast chicken 34–5
  salmon parcels 144
  sausage and mash 92
  smoked mackerel Niçoise 142
  10 minute fish cakes 139
  tikka lamb chops 118
prawns: griddled prawns with lemony green bean salad 135
  quick prawn curry 134

Q

quesadillas, chipotle steak and cheese 66

R

ragu, duck 45
ratatouille 166
  ratatouille and pasta soup 168
rice 11
  easy arancini 136
  egg fried rice with garlic broccoli 70
  seafood paella 136
  spicy stir-fried beef 68
ricotta: roast butternut squash dip 148
  roast butternut squash with ricotta and rocket on gnocchi 148

S

salads: Asian chicken salad 14
  Asian slaw 62
  belly pork salad with spicy sesame dressing 88
  griddled prawns with lemony green bean salad 135
  lamb and feta salad 120
  Lebanese style chickpea salad 156
  Mexican salad 157
  miso aubergine salad 154
  Moroccan salad 22
  smoked mackerel Niçoise 142
  steak and roasted red pepper salad 57
  tofu and cucumber salad 158
  Vietnamese duck salad 47
  warm lamb salad 108
salmon: salmon parcels 144
  simple salmon pâté 145
salt n' pepper tofu 160
sandwiches: BBQ beef rib sandwich 67
  chicken sandwiches 36
  hot beef sandwich 78
  lamb, feta and hummus pitta 127
  Philly cheesesteak sandwich 56
  pork sandwich with quick apple sauce 89
  satay pork sandwich 103
satay pork sandwich 103
sausages: breakfast hash 92
  leek and pea Glamorgan sausages 150
  pork and split pea soup 104
  quick cassoulet 98

sausage and lentil stew 93
  sausage and mash 92
  sausage and mustard pasta 93
  sausage meatballs and pasta 96
  see also chorizo
seafood paella 136
shepherd's pie 110
smoked mackerel: smoked mackerel pâté with a kick 142
  smoked mackerel Niçoise 142
smoked salmon: creamy smoked salmon pasta 143
  Nordic smoked salmon 143
smokey duck breast with griddled asparagus 46
soups: chicken soup 38
  chickpea and potato soup, spicy 156
  chorizo and sweet potato soup 90
  pho 80
  pork and split pea soup 104
  ratatouille and pasta soup 168
  spring broth with lamb 117
spaghetti: spag bol 76
  spaghetti and meatballs 64
  spaghetti carbonara 94
spices 8
spinach: chicken saag curry 18
  duck, feta and spinach filo pie 50
split peas: pork and split pea soup 104
spring broth with lamb 117
spring onions: griddled spring onion tart 162
squash see butternut squash
steak and roasted red pepper salad 57
stews: one-pot lamb stew 116
  sausage and lentil stew 93
  slow-cooked lamb shanks with olives and polenta 123
sticky toffee mug cakes 184
sticky toffee popcorn 174
storage 10–11
strawberries: cheesecake 178
sugar 9
swede: maple-glazed gammon steak 94
sweet chilli pork stir fry with black fungus 86
sweet potatoes: chilli sweet potato wedges 28
  chorizo and sweet potato soup 90
  five-spice duck legs with chilli sweet potato mash 42

miso steak and chilli sweet potato 66

T

tarts: artichoke heart, basil and mozzarella tart 164
  griddled spring onion tart 162
teriyaki nachos 17
Thai lentil dhal 151
tikka lamb chops 118
toast: cinnamon toast 183
  horseradish toasts 57
toffee sauce 184
tofu: salt n' pepper tofu 160
  tofu and cucumber salad 158
tomatoes: aubergine and tomato fusilli 152
  chicken saag curry 18
  duck ragu 45
  mussel linguine 140
  ratatouille 166
  sausage meatballs and pasta 96
  slow-cooked lamb shanks with olives and polenta 123
  spag bol 76
  tomato sauce 64
tortillas: chipotle steak and cheese quesadillas 66
  veggie fajitas 157

V

vegetables: ratatouille 166
  spring broth with lamb 117
  see also aubergines, peppers etc
veggie fajitas 157
Vietnamese duck salad 47
vinegars 8

W

wine: duck ragu 45
  sausage and lentil stew 93
  slow-cooked lamb shanks with olives and polenta 123
wraps: chicken liver wrap 23
  kofta wrap 112
  lettuce wraps with shredded duck and hoisin sauce 42
  Nordic smoked salmon 143
  veggie fajitas 157

ACKNOWLEDGEMENTS

A huge thank you to all these lovely people...

For making the book look beautiful: Céline Hughes, Gemma Hayden, Helen Lewis, Lisa Linder, Fiona Kennedy, Emily Jonzen, Polly Webb-Wilson, Aya Nishimura.

For help and amazing support: Felicity Blunt, Emma Herdman and Jane O'Shea.

To my family and friends: Dad for being chief taster and general hero. My sister Polly and brother Tom for always being there for me. My terrific tasters Yuley and Louise. Mickey, the cat, helpfully cleaning up anything I dropped on the floor.

In memory of my wonderful mum, who gave me the love of food and constantly inspired and supported me in every way. You are missed and thought of every day, especially when I'm in the kitchen. This is for you.

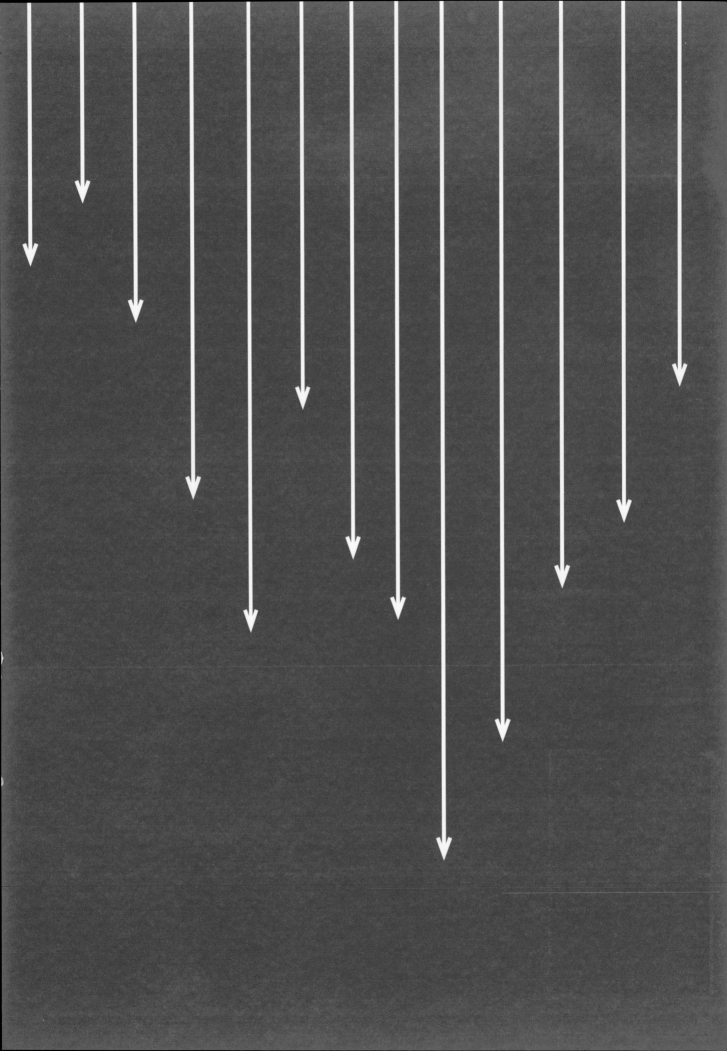